HANNIBAL

LEADERSHIP ▪ STRATEGY ▪ CONFLICT

NIC FIELDS ▪ ILLUSTRATED BY PETER DENNIS

First published in 2010 by Osprey Publishing
Midland House, West Way, Botley, Oxford OX2 0PH, UK
44-02 23rd St, Suite 219, Long Island City, NY 11101, USA

E-mail: info@ospreypublishing.com

ISBN: 978 1 84908 349 2
E-book ISBN: 978 1 84908 350 8

Editorial by Ilios Publishing Ltd, Oxford, UK (www.iliospublishing.com)
Page layout by Myriam Bell Design, France
Index by Alison Worthington
Typeset in Stone Serif and Officina Sans
Maps by The Mapping Specialists Ltd.
Originated by PPS Grasmere Ltd, Leeds, UK
Printed in China through Worldprint Ltd

10 11 12 13 14   10 9 8 7 6 5 4 3 2 1

Artist's note

Readers may care to note that the original paintings from which the
colour plates in this book were prepared are available for private sale.
All reproduction copyright whatsoever is retained by the Publishers.
All enquiries should be addressed to:

Peter Dennis, Fieldhead, The Park, Mansfield, Notts, NG18 2AT

The Publishers regret that they can enter into no correspondence upon
this matter.

Front cover picture credit

Mary Evans Picture Library.

The Woodland Trust

Osprey Publishing are supporting the Woodland Trust, the UK's leading
woodland conservation charity, by funding the dedication of trees.

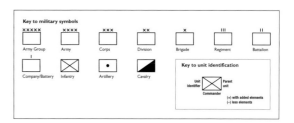

CONTENTS

INTRODUCTION

Hannibal beim Überqueren der Alpen. Military historians have agreed that as a feat of leadership and endurance Alexander's crossing of the majestic snow-capped ranges of the Hindu Kush ('Killer of Hindus') early in 329 BC far surpasses Hannibal's crossing of the Alps late in 218 BC. Alexander, however, never took on Rome. (Author's collection)

Let us begin our story with an amusing Hannibalic anecdote. As the armies were deploying to commit themselves to the lottery of battle, it is commonly said that Antiochos of Syria turned to Hannibal Barca, the luckless-but-bewitching Carthaginian general who accompanied his entourage, to enquire whether his army, its ranks gleaming with silver and gold, its commanders grandly arrayed in their weighty jewels and rich silks, would be enough for the Romans. 'Indeed they will be more than enough', sneered Hannibal, 'even though the Romans are the greediest nation on earth' (Aulus Gellius *Noctes Atticae* 5.5). Such a story, and others like it, makes him easy to remember, but of course it is an oversimplification; one or two vivid strokes with a pen do not delineate a man. Still, the Carthaginians certainly have, in our modern eyes at least, the romantic glamour of the doomed. The Romans had reduced their city to a heap of ashes and destroyed their culture at a time when middle-republican Rome was the aggressive bully of the Mediterranean world. Yet nothing is inevitable in history, and the Carthaginians put up far more resistance than any of the magnificent Hellenistic kingdoms, and came close, during the second in a series of three wars, to destroying Roman power completely.

Their commander-in-chief during this titanic struggle – as one might guess – was the cool, self-contained, locked-in hero Hannibal (247–183 BC), the eldest son of the charismatic general Hamilcar Barca (d. 229 BC), and, for my money at least, the greatest general of antiquity. Everybody has an opinion, not least the magnificent man himself. Though he rated himself as third after Alexander the Great and Pyrrhos of Epeiros (Livy 35.14.5–8, cf. Plutarch

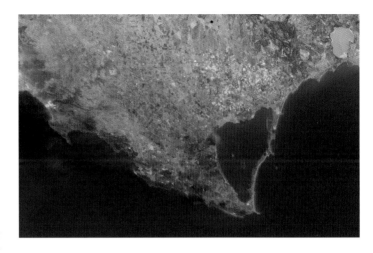

Flamininus 21.3), Hannibal was overly modest. His victories were certainly far more impressive than those of Pyrrhos were – crushing as opposed to Pyrrhic – and his strategic focus was clearer. Though Alexander achieved spectacular conquests, he did so using the superb royal army inherited from his father, Philip II of Macedon, whereas Hannibal achieved his continuous run of successes with an ad hoc collection of polyglot mercenaries who were fighting with a variety of motivations. Given that, neither Pyrrhos nor Hannibal made decisive use of their elephants; for the Carthaginian they figure only in his earliest battles, the Tagus (220 BC) and the Trebbia (218 BC), and then, finally, at Zama (202 BC). On the other hand, Hannibal was a cavalry master, the great Alexander's equal. Here, however, his tactics were clearly not modelled on those of Alexander, who preferred penetration as his tactical means rather than encirclement. Hannibal always kept in mind one of the most basic battle lessons – never attack your enemy directly when you can outflank him. Likewise, whereas Pyrrhos shone brilliantly as a Homeric Achilles in combat, Hannibal was a consummate trickster, a shape-shifter, more of an Odysseus. He was master of ambushes, of cunning battle plans and false missives.

Squatting on a peninsula commanding one of the finest harbours in the Mediterranean, New Carthage – presumably called *Qart-Hadasht* by the Carthaginians, like their mother city – had been founded by Hasdrubal the Splendid to serve as the capital of Punic Iberia. This is a NASA screenshot of Puerto de Cartenga and Cap de Pals. (NASA)

There are two models of ancient military strategy. Hannibal was a warrior chief like Pyrrhos, but there were fundamental differences between the two of them. If Pyrrhos chose the way of Achilles, the way of honour and violence, then Hannibal chose the way of Odysseus, the way of guile and expediency. Occidental minds prefer the spirit of Achilles: bittersweet, ferocious and brilliant. Little wonder, therefore, that modern commentators have been too quick to condemn Hannibal, criticizing his strategy for failing to comprehend the nature of the Roman-led confederation – the daring individual braving Leviathan with a lance – and for failing to ensure that adequate reinforcements came either by sea from Africa or land from Iberia. Yet there is no doubt that his invasion was the only way that Carthage could ever have defeated Rome. Naturally he had counted on a simultaneous uprising against Rome by the imperfectly subjugated Italian peninsula. He was right about the Celts, but almost entirely wrong about the Etruscans and the Greeks, who in the end preferred Rome to their longstanding enemy of Carthage. With the heart of Italy refusing to back Hannibal, his long-term strategy was not going to be a success. In fact he overestimated the spirit of rebellion against Rome, and here he was perhaps five decades too late, and to many Italic peoples there was more reason to identify with Rome than against it. The evidence from negotiations between Hannibal and those who

did defect (mainly Samnites, once fierce enemies of Rome) shows that what they really wanted was autonomy and the chance to determine their own fate. Defection to Hannibal, who was after all an outsider, was changing one master for another, or so many feared.

So he was right or he was wrong. It depends, like the blind men describing an elephant, on what part of the beast you touch. Yet whatever one's opinions, the audacity of the march from Iberia to Italy, crossing both the Pyrenees and the Alps, remains breathtaking, and we should not underestimate how near his designs came to success. Hannibal's 15-day march over the Alps in late October or early November 218 BC makes epic reading. Even in Livy's hostile narrative the Carthaginian general emerges as its hero – rather like Satan in Milton's *Paradise Lost* – though in part this was done to justify the defeats Rome suffered at his hands. Hannibal had done the unexpected and was now poised to bring Rome to its knees. He was also a commander who was about to enter the pages of history.

Hannibal Crossing the Mighty Alps, colour illustration by Dudley C. Tennant (*fl.* 1898–1918) for *Newnes' Pictorial Book of Knowledge* (*c.*1920). Scholars, scientists and sleuths may argue about where the exact Alpine pass was, and will argue as long as Hannibal is remembered, but his passage of the Alps, along with the charge of the Light Brigade and Custer's last stand, has stirred the imagination of humankind. (The Bridgeman Art Library)

THE EARLY YEARS

Telling the story of Hannibal is difficult from the very beginning. Hannibal, who was born shortly before or after his father's departure for Sicily (247 BC), probably never saw him until he returned to Carthage after the First Punic War was over (241 BC). Nevertheless, the absentee parent apparently ensured his son had a good education that included a strong Greek element. Later, Hannibal was to take Greek historians with him on his expedition, including the Spartan Sosylos, his former tutor who had taught him Greek, and the Sicilian Silenos, though in what capacity he had taught the young Hannibal we do not know (Nepos *Hannibal* 13.3, cf. Cicero *de oratore* 2.18.75, Vegetius 3 praef. 62). He established himself as something of a literary lion, even to the extent of having written books in Greek, including one addressed to the Rhodians on the Anatolian campaigns of Cnaeus Manlius Vulso (Nepos *Hannibal* 13.3). His Greek training made him intellectually the superior of any of the Roman commanders (excepting Scipio, perhaps) he was to face upon the field of conflict.

Having learnt the art of scholarship, Hannibal then spent the rest of his youth in Iberia learning the trades of war and politics by his father's side (Zonaras 8.21). As an adolescent, then, Hannibal was set on his life's path, serving under Hasdrubal the Splendid, his brother-in-law, as his second-in-command-cum-cavalry-commander (Livy 21.4.3–5, 8, Appian *Iberica* 6, Nepos *Hannibal* 3.1). Though obviously not a Greek, either ethnically or culturally, the young Hannibal was fully exposed to the military traditions of the Greeks as well as those of his ancestral Semitic culture. We must imagine him as a good all-round athlete and good at all the arts that would make him a successful warrior, it being generally believed that those who excelled in athletic games and the like would naturally distinguish themselves in war.

When the highly competent Polybios came to analyse the causes of the second war between Rome and Carthage, he was undoubtedly right to put first what he calls the 'the wrath [*thymós*] of Hamilcar' (3.9.6), his anger at the end of the first war when he was forced to surrender despite remaining undefeated in Sicily. Polybios later justifies his view that Hamilcar's bitter attitude contributed towards the outbreak of war, which only began ten years after his death, by telling the celebrated tale of Hannibal's oath. The oath, pledged at the temple of Baal Shamaim, the 'Lord of the Heavens', to his father before their departure to Iberia in 237 BC, was 'never to show goodwill to the Romans' (3.11.7). At the time Hannibal was just nine years old.

A stretch of the fortification walls (Greek below, Roman above) of Emporion (Latin Emporiae, now Ampurias), a daughter foundation of Greek Massalia (Massilia in Latin, now Marseille) and a stage in Phocaean littoral exploration. (David Mateos García)

The story has inevitably been doubted, but Polybios says that Hannibal himself told it to Antiochos of Syria some 40 years later when he was serving the king, who was bogged down in a war with Rome, as a military adviser. The view that the Second Punic War was thus a war of revenge certainly gained widespread credence among the Romans, and revenge is part of war, as the Romans knew (e.g. Livy 21.1.4–5, 5.1, Nepos *Hannibal* 2.3–6). This is admirably encapsulated in a Roman anecdote, as related by Valerius Maximus, in which Hamilcar, watching his three sons playing together, proudly exclaimed: 'These are the lion cubs I am rearing for the destruction of Rome!' (9.3.2). This was the war the Romans, who were in no doubt about its instigator, often referred to as 'Hannibal's War'.

Yet this notion of revenge is, perhaps, most dramatically expressed by Virgil when he has the Carthaginian queen Dido, heartbroken and furious at her desertion by Aeneas, curse him and his whole race and calls upon an 'unknown avenger [to] harry the race of Dardanus with fire and sword wherever they may settle, now and in the future' (*Aeneid* 4.626–7 West). She then fell on Aeneas' sword and killed herself. With such artistry did Virgil introduce Hannibal into his epic without naming him. Be that as it may, it would seem that all the leading officers swore the oath, not just Hannibal, and the oath they swore was not vengeance on Rome but a promise never to be 'a friend of Rome'. This is important phraseology: in those days the term 'a friend of Rome' implied a vassal of Rome.

'Hannibal, whilst even yet a child, swears eternal hatred to the Romans', a cartoon by John Leach (1817–64) from *The Comic History of Rome* (c.1850). It is said that in men of high purpose, the seed of all their future endeavours is sown in their earliest years. The oath is still as fruitful a topic of debate as it was in Polybios' day. (John Leach)

Eryx (Monte San Giuliano), looking north-north-east from the Mozia quay. In 244 BC, using the Eryx's flat summit as a base, Hamilcar Barca opened guerrilla operations against the Romans on Sicily, diversified with naval raids along the Italian coastline. For the few remaining years of the First Punic War, he was to remain a constant thorn in the side of Rome. (Fields-Carré Collection)

Hannibal's march across the Alps

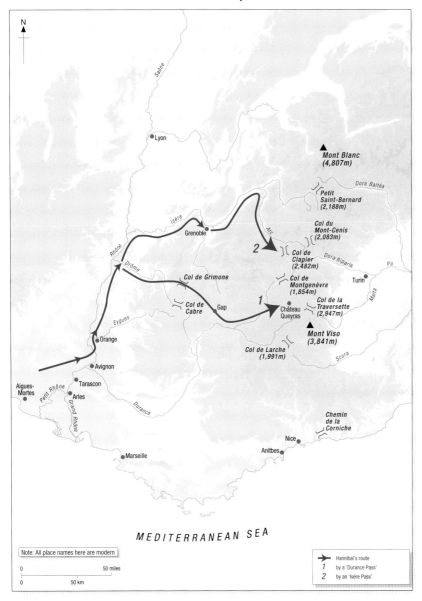

N

Lyon

Mont Blanc
(4,807m)

Dora Baltéa

Petit
Saint-Bernard
(2,188m)

Col du
Mont-Cenis
(2,083m)

Saône

Isère

Grenoble

Arc

2

Col de
Clapier
(2,482m)

Dora Riparia

Po

Rhône

Drôme

Col de Grimone

Col de
Montgenèvre
(1,854m)

Turin

Col de
Cabre

Gap

1

Château
Queyras

Col de la
Traversette
(2,947m)

Malta

Eygues

Orange

Mont Viso
(3,841m)

Col de Larche
(1,991m)

Scura

Avignon

Aigues-
Mortes

Tarascon

Arles

Durance

Chemin
de la
Corniche

Petit Rhône

Grand Rhône

Marseille

Nice

Anitbes

MEDITERRANEAN SEA

Note: All place names here are modern

0   50 miles

0   50 km

→ Hannibal's route
1 by a 'Durance Pass'
2 by an 'Isère Pass'

It was in Sicily that Hamilcar had successfully maintained a struggle against the Roman forces in the north-western corner of the island until the Punic defeat at sea left him no alternative but to open negotiations, the Carthaginian government having given him full powers to handle the situation. During this twilight period of the conflict, Hamilcar, whom Polybios considered the ablest commander on either side 'both in daring and in genius' (1.64.6), and even the elder Cato held in the highest regard (Plutarch *Cato major* 8.14), displayed his talent in low-level raiding, skirmishing and ambushing. He had the art, which he transmitted to his eldest son, of binding to himself the mercenary armies of the state by a close personal tie that was proof against all temptation.

THE MILITARY LIFE

It is true that neither Hamilcar himself, nor his immediate successor in Iberia, his son-in-law Hasdrubal the Splendid, made any overt move against Rome. The magnificent and charismatic Hasdrubal continued the policy of Hamilcar but with added flair, and largely increased the Punic influence in Iberia. In fact, Rome, probably after having been prodded by its Greek ally Massalia, eventually woke up to this new danger, and in 226 BC Hasdrubal signed what has entered Anglophone historical writing as the Ebro Treaty, which defined spheres of influence in the Iberian peninsula by preventing the Carthaginians from crossing 'the Iber bearing arms' (Polybios 2.13.7, cf. 3.30.3). It could be argued of course that this treaty was practical recognition of Hasdrubal's supreme position in Punic Iberia, and implicit Roman acceptance of further Punic expansion across most of the peninsula, though in the view of our sole source on this matter, namely Polybios (2.22.9–11), it was the return of the Gaulish peril that prompted Rome to act as it did. Yet we do not know how much these two gentlemen influenced the young Hannibal, and it is his attitude that is important. Telling is his forthright attack upon Saguntum (219 BC), a town that he knew to be under Rome's protection less than two years after he succeeded to the supreme command of the Punic forces in Iberia (Polybios 3.30.1, cf. Livy 21.2.7). Here Polybios uses the Greek word *pistis*, which corresponds (roughly) to the Latin *fides*, meaning 'good faith'. Under traditional Roman policy, if a community handed itself over completely to Roman *fides* it entrusted itself to Rome absolutely, but without specific obligations (i.e. as most of Rome's allies had done).

Located on the eastern extremity of a narrow, high rocky plateau reaching out to the coast – at the time Polybios was writing, it was a little over a kilometre from the sea – Saguntum was an Iberian town, perhaps with some Greek admixture, halfway between New Carthage and the river Iber.

According to Livy (21.7.2) Saguntum (Sagunto) was regarded as a Greek colony founded by citizens of Zakynthos (Zante), but this appears to be a fable born of the resemblance of the two place names. Hannibal captured Saguntum after an eight-month siege (219 BC), and Rome, like many nations since, started a war on trumped-up charges. This is a general view of the later, medieval fortifications. (Bridgeman Art Library)

Certainly before 220 BC Hannibal had left the town untouched in order not to provoke the Romans before he was ready (Polybios 3.14.10). Telling also is the bold and decisive way in which he matured his plans for the invasion of Italy. Together, it at least suggests Hannibal was not too unwilling to have war with Rome. Alternatively, we can easily accuse the Romans of double-dealing as Saguntum lay far south of the Iber. If the terms of the Ebro Treaty prevented them from crossing the river under arms, as it did the Carthaginians, they could hardly come to the aid of Saguntum. In any case, the Romans claimed that the alliance with this town overrode the treaty, and the Carthaginians claimed that the same agreement allowed them to attack Saguntum (Polybios 3.21.1, 29.1–3, 30.3).

As usual Polybios pulls no punches, for he has an unambiguous view that the Saguntum episode was a mere pretext. As he had earlier pointed out to his Greek readers, those Roman historians who have tried to identify the causes of the war between Rome and Carthage with Hannibal's laying siege to Saguntum and his subsequent crossing of the Iber had got it all wrong. And still to this day the juridical controversy over the responsibility of the war is discussed, fruitlessly for the most part, by many scholars. What Polybios does concede, however, is that 'these events might be described as the *beginnings* of the war' (3.6.2). Thus our Greek soldier-historian has a clear view that the Saguntum episode was a mere pretext.

Hannibal's long-term objective was fairly straightforward, namely to turn Italy, rather than Iberia, into the 'field of blood'. From his father he had learnt that it was inadvisable to be bogged down in a slogging match with Rome. If Polybios (2.24.16) is to be believed, Rome and its confederate allies had a manpower resource of some 700,000 infantry and 70,000 cavalry. No matter how many times Hannibal knocked out a Roman army, Rome could delve into its human reserves and another would stubbornly take its place. He, on the contrary, knew that he must save men, for in a war of attrition he would have no hope. Hannibal, knowing that over half of Rome's forces

The first stage of Hannibal's long march took him across the Iber (Latin Iberus, now the Ebro) and into southern Gaul. Across the river was 'bandit' country, and Hannibal had to subdue some tribes and storm several settlements, all at the cost of considerable loss to his own army. This is a view of the Ebro delta near Ruimar, Catalonia. (Till F. Teenck)

Reference to Hannibal's wintering at Capua (Santa Maria di Capua Vetere) as rich, luxurious and lazy is commonplace among moralists. The story goes that by lingering there his cause was lost (e.g. Livy 23.45.4, 'Capua was Hannibal's Cannae'). True, the city was the western capital of copiousness and opulence, but lax living was not really the root of Hannibal's problems. (Fototeca ENIT)

were furnished by its allies, deliberately set out to strangle this supply of manpower by claiming the Italic peoples would be freed from the Roman yoke. It is for this reason that he had to invade Italy, as distant rumours of Punic victories would not convince Rome's allies to switch sides.

The execution of the objective was, on the other hand, far from simple. Hannibal could invade Italy from the sea, a much faster and easier task than marching there by land. However, without bases in Sicily, even southern Italy was at the limit of operational range for a fleet of oared warships operating from Africa, and Carthaginian naval power in Iberia was not great. Carthaginian naval capability had in fact never been fully restored after the shattering defeats suffered in the first war, either in numbers or morale, therefore another stumbling block to the maritime option was Rome's superior naval strength, 220 seaworthy quinqueremes to Carthage's 105, 50 of which were stationed in Iberia (Polybios 3.33.4, 41.2, Livy 21.17.3, 22.4, 49.2, 4). And so, with Carthage outmatched, and perhaps outclassed, on the high seas, the risk of a seaborne invasion was too great for Hannibal to take. The next logical step, especially if you are based in Iberia, is to invade via Gaul, and thus Hannibal needed to march across the Alps.

On the summit: Hannibal enters Italy

Mountains, as Alexander proved, and as Hannibal was to prove just over a century later, provide no defence against armies that are resolute in their pursuit of an objective. Mountains defend nothing but themselves. The Swiss military strategist Jomini wrote: 'It has long been a question whether the possession of the mountains gave control of the valleys, or whether possession of the valleys gave control of the mountains' (*Précis de l' art de la guerre*, chapter III, article XXVIII). Indeed, mountains, like rivers and deserts, have never served as fixed military frontiers in history, but, as Lucien Febvre once observed, 'they are promoted to the dignity of a natural frontier' by victorious nations in the process of expansion and in the desire to define space (1970: 325–31). Thus Napoleon could scribble, 'The frontiers of states are either large rivers, or chains of mountains, or deserts' (*Military Maxims* I). Of course, seen from afar on a clear day, the towering Alps must have appeared an impressive barrier.

Having reached the summit of his Alpine crossing, Hannibal rested his battered and frostbitten army for a couple of days. It was then, at this desolate seam in the universe, while the survivors took breath and the stragglers caught up, that he took the opportunity to hearten his exhausted and dispirited men. 'Hannibal therefore directed his men's gaze towards the plains of the Po, and reminded them of the welcome they would receive from the Gauls who inhabited them. At the same time he pointed out the direction of Rome itself, and in this way he did something to restore their confidence' (Polybios 3.54.4).

We see Hannibal ideally dressed for a journey into the high Alps. He has wrapped himself in the pelt of a brown bear, the grain side turned outwards, and wears Gaulish long trousers of sheep's wool, picked out with a variegated small check pattern. These are tucked into Gaulish ankle boots, which are made from the hide of mature cattle. Around his legs are wrappings of fur, predominately from red or roe deer. He wears a bearskin cap and has grown what is now an enormous beard.

Tarentum sat upon a slender promontory stretching from east to west between an outer bay (Mare Grande) and an inner lagoon (Mare Piccolo). Between the western extremity and the mainland opposite was a narrow sound, which was overlooked by the citadel as it ran north into the lagoon. This magnificent body of water, some 26km in circumference, provided the best harbour in southern Italy. (Fototeca ENIT)

Confident in its command of the sea, the Senate's plan for the conduct of the war was simple and direct. The two consuls for the year were to operate separately and offensively; one was to go to Iberia to face Hannibal across the Iber, whilst the other was to go to Sicily to prepare an invasion of Africa and confront the Carthaginians in their own backyard (Polybios 3.40.2, 41.2, Livy 21.17.5, 8). Each would take with him the now standard consular army of two legions and two *alae* from the Latin and Italian allies, the *socii*. A further two legions, each under a praetor and supported by a Latin-Italian *ala*, would be stationed in Gallia Cisalpina, which was only half conquered and needed a garrison, but that was a local matter. The war would be fought aggressively and overseas.

To the utter surprise and consternation of the Romans, Hannibal crossed the Iber and then proceeded to march over the Alps – his exact route is still a matter of fierce debate – during the late autumn of 218 BC. He then proceeded to defeat one Roman army after another in a series of three brilliant victories: the Trebbia, Lake Trasimene and Cannae. All this should act as a salutary reminder to us, namely that when embarking on a war no one knows exactly what is going to happen. As one of Euripides' characters remarks: 'Whenever war comes to the vote of the people, no one reckons on his own death – that misfortune he thinks will happen to someone else' (*Supplicant Women* 481–3). In the dog days of August 216 BC we can reckon that nobody on the streets of Rome anticipated the carrion field of Cannae.

The immediate result of these Roman disasters was that practically all of southern Italy, excepting the Latin colonies and Greek cities, came over to Hannibal. Following the time-honoured practice of rushing to the aid of the victor, this was a series of political events that began with the defection of Capua (216 BC), the capital of Campania and second only to Rome itself in size and prosperity, and would finish with the capitulation of Tarentum (212 BC), the third-largest city of Italy. Though the citadel remained in the hands of the small Roman garrison, possession of the city itself gave Hannibal access to a magnificent seaport. The capitulation of Tarentum was immediately followed by that of three other Greek cities, namely Metapontion, Thourioi and Herakleia, and so the whole coastline of the instep of Italy passed into Carthaginian control (Livy 25.15.7, Appian *Hannibalica* 35). Hannibal must have been confident that he was now on the high road to success. Perhaps there would be a little more fighting, but the war was in the bag.

THE HOUR OF DESTINY

It need occasion no surprise that Hannibal had learnt his professionalism and confidence as a fighting soldier from his father, and there is more than a hint of Hamilcar, albeit on a grander scale, in his son's ability to maintain himself and his colourful army in a foreign land for so many years. It is possible that he also inherited the plan for invading Italy (just as Alexander inherited Philip's plan for invading Asia), for his father had raided the southern Italian coast 'devastating the territory of Locri and the Bruttii' (Polybios 1.56.3), hoping both to bring the Italic peoples to revolt against Rome and to keep its forces busy.

It was Hamilcar who, because of his swiftness in war, was the first to be given the surname Barca, *bârâq*, the Semitic word for lightning flash, and his brilliant progeny was not only to honour the new family moniker, but also, it frequently seemed, to be actually capable of channelling this elemental energy like a current. It was the Roman Florus who justly, and poetically, compared Hannibal and his army to a thunderbolt, which 'burst its way through the midst of the Alps and swooped down upon Italy from those snows of fabulous heights like a missile hurled from the skies' (*Epitome*

Hannibal's march from Iberia to Italy

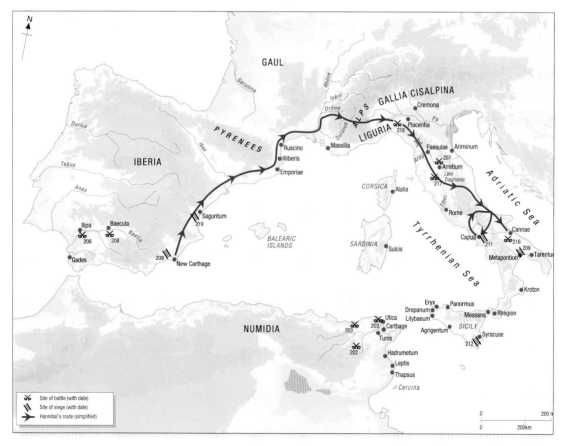

Battle of the Trebbia, December 218 BC

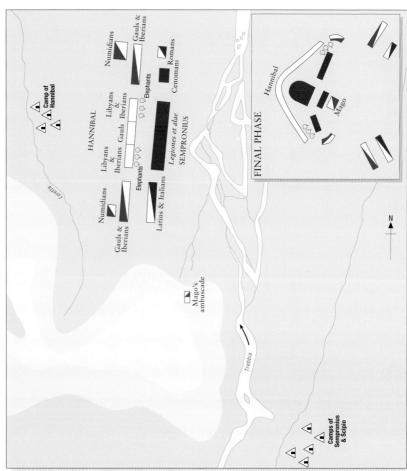

The Trebbia, a meandering tributary of the Po near Placentia (Piacenza), with its high scrub-covered banks. It was on a bitter December morning that the Roman army was led breakfastless through the swollen icy waters of this river against Hannibal. His plan was for his centre to hold firm and his wings to outflank and defeat the cold, wet and hungry enemy, while his brother Mago, who lay in ambush in an arboraceous gully, charged the enemy's rear. Two-thirds of the Roman army was destroyed. (Davide Papalini)

1.22.9). His reputation as a tactician has survived intact to this day, unlike his reputation as a strategist. His strategy was clearly ambitious, but it would be wrong to conclude with the modern consensus that our supercharged Carthaginian could not have won. If Hannibal had learned his battle tactics from his father, as a military strategist he was in a class all his own.

The Trebbia, December 218 BC

Hannibal had come over the Alps to Gallia Cisalpina, won a large-scale cavalry skirmish on the Ticinus (Ticino), and in a cold, snowy mid-December was camped on the west bank of the Trebbia close to its confluence with the Po, south-west of Placentia. Over on the east bank were the Roman consuls, Tiberius Sempronius Longus and Publius Cornelius Scipio, with four legions and, perhaps, six Latin-Italian *alae*. They also had the support of the Cenomani, the only Gallic tribe in northern Italy to remain loyal. Scipio was recovering from a severe wound and temporarily *hors de combat*, but his colleague was all out for giving battle and Hannibal was aware of this. So he set out deliberately to lure Sempronius into a trap on the flat, open terrain between the two camps.

The land west of the Trebbia is wide, flat and treeless, yet Hannibal, during a personal reconnaissance, had located a watercourse crossing the open country and running between two steep and heavily overgrown banks. Laying behind and south of where he expected to lure the Romans to fight a pitched battle, it was in the low scrub and other flora of this natural feature that he set an ambush under the command of his young brother Mago (Polybios 3.71.9). The day before the expected encounter, a picked force of 1,000 infantry and 1,000 cavalry, mostly Numidian, was formed for this vital task. Under the cover of darkness Mago inserted his men into the ambush position, where they were completely hidden from the view of the Romans. The stage was thus set for the first major confrontation of Hannibal's war.

Polybios says (3.72.11–13) that the Roman army contained 16,000 Roman and 20,000 Latin-Italian infantry, and 4,000 cavalry (demoralized by their recent trouncing at the Ticinus), while Livy (21.55.4) adds a contingent (of doubtful value) from the Cenomani. Scipio's wound obliged him to pass overall command over to Sempronius. If the figures given for Hannibal's army are correct, and if Mago's 2,000 men are to be added to the total, the Carthaginian army had been swelled by more than 14,000 Gauls – 9,000 infantry and 5,000 cavalry – for Hannibal had entered the Italian peninsula with only 20,000 infantry (Libyans and Iberians) and 6,000 Iberian and Numidian cavalry (Polybios 3.56.4).

After the battle of the Trebbia, Hannibal left the Po Valley and crossed the Apennines, probably via the Col de Collina (952m). This brought his army down into the valley of the Arno (Latin Arnus), a marshy swamp after the snowmelt and spring rains. This is a view of the Arno as it flows through Florence. (Fields-Carré Collection)

He also commanded, we guess, some 30 or so elephants, having started his epic journey with 37 of these rather risky weapons (Appian *Hannibalica* 1.4, cf. Polybios 3.42.10).

At first light the following morning – Polybios says (3.72.3) the day was near the winter solstice – Hannibal's Numidian horsemen mounted and crossed the river to skirmish around the Roman outposts and provoke Sempronius into premature action, while the rest of the Carthaginian army stayed by their campfires to eat a hearty breakfast and rub their bodies with olive oil to keep out the biting cold (Polybios 3.72.6, Livy 21.55.1). Sempronius reacted just as Hannibal had hoped, sending all his cavalry out against the audacious Numidians, closely followed by some 6,000 *velites*. The consul, eager to engage, then gave orders for his legionaries to stand to arms and prepare to march out against the enemy, thereby giving them little or no time to take their morning meal. At this point the raiders, following their strict instructions, began to give way and gradually retire towards the river. The bait had been taken.

When the Romans proceeded to cross the river, ice-cold and swollen breast-high by recent rain, Hannibal threw forward 8,000 lightly armed troops to support the Numidians and form a screen behind which his army could safely deploy. Then, and only then, his main body left the camp and advanced a little over a kilometre (Polybios 3.72.8), where they fell into a line of battle. This was formed by a single line of infantry, Libyans and Iberians 20,000 strong, with his new Gaulish allies in the centre, and his 10,000 cavalry, including the rallied Numidians, equally divided on each flank. Hannibal also divided his elephants, and probably stationed them in front of the two wings of his infantry line (Polybios 3.72.9, cf. Livy 21.55.2).

Having struggled across the river, Sempronius deployed his legionaries, now half frozen, completely soaked and very hungry, in the customary battle formation, the *triplex acies*, with the 4,000 cavalry, now recalled from their fruitless but fatiguing pursuit of the Numidians, and the Cenomani on their flanks (Polybios 3.72.11, Livy 21.55.4). During what must have been a long and drawn-out process, more so as the army was uncommonly large (in effect, a double-consular army) and relatively inexperienced, the snow of that frigid morning turned to driving sleet and rain.

The battle opened with the usual exchanges between the skirmishers of both sides, and here the Romans were soon at a disadvantage. Not only were the *velites* outnumbered, but they had already been engaged with Hannibal's Numidian horsemen and thus expended much of their missile supply. After a short engagement, therefore, they fell back through the intervals between the maniples, and Sempronius, who remained full of

Flaminius broke camp at Arretium and pressed after Hannibal along the road from Cortona to Perusia. At the north-western angle of Lake Trasimene (Lago Trasimeno), seen here from Fortezza di Girifalco Cortona, he made camp, intending to pursue his march along the northern shore the next day. At that time the shore was not as it is now, having receded as the result of alluvial deposits and canalization works. (Fields-Carré Collection)

confidence and was still in an offensive mood, ordered a general advance. At this point, Hannibal, taking advantage of his superiority in this particular arm, let loose his cavalry.

The Roman cavalry, heavily outnumbered and already haggard from chasing the agile Numidians, gave way at the first shock of these fresh troops, broke and fled in rout for the river, with the Iberian and Gaulish cavalry in merciless pursuit. The Numidians coming up behind, however, at once swung inwards upon the exposed flanks of the legionaries just as the elephants and lightly armed troops similarly engaged them. At this point Sempronius realized, probably, that he was no longer on the offensive.

The Roman infantry, despite their cold and hunger, had managed to hold their own with Hannibal's infantry and might have prevailed. Then the elephants, in cooperation with the lightly armed troops, began to attack the Roman centre. It was at this point that Mago, timing his attack to a nicety, sprung his ambush and charged into the Roman rear. Thereupon, at last, Sempronius' command began to break up (Polybios 3.74.1). Still, some 10,000 legionaries in the centre of the first and second lines (namely, the *hastati* and the *princeps*), refusing to accept defeat, hacked their way through the Gauls who made up Hannibal's centre. Then, seeing that all was lost and that a return across the swollen river to their camp was completely cut off, they marched off in good order and made their escape to the walls of Placentia. Hannibal made no attempt to stop them. His men were weary and his victory was assured.

Though we do not have a figure for the Roman losses, the rest of the Roman army must have suffered heavily in the rout towards the river. Likewise, the sources are vague for Hannibal's casualties, although Polybios says (3.74.11) that the heaviest losses were suffered by the Gauls in the centre. Moreover, in the cold snap that followed the battle, many of his men and horses and all but one of the elephants died.

Lake Trasimene, June 217 BC

Hannibal had lost the sight of one of his eyes while travelling through the wetlands around the river Arno. By then he had also lost almost all his elephants. Yet the Carthaginian general, the consummate trickster, had never envisaged a decisive role for elephants in his cunning battle plans. And so, at Lake Trasimene in Etruria, his one eye still clear-sighted enough to outwit another Roman consul and his army, Hannibal made use of a novel ruse. The battle was to be an ambush on a grand scale, one of those rare instances in the annals of military history in which a whole army lies in wait and then destroys almost the whole of the opposition.

Hannibal's spectacular ambush and defeat of Flaminius' consular army took place somewhere along the northern shore of Lake Trasimene, seen here from Castiglione del Lago. By entering the narrow space between the hillside and the water, the unsuspecting Romans were doomed from the very outset. In Rome a praetor was to announce laconically: 'We have been beaten in a great battle' (Livy 22.7.8). Darker days were yet to come. (Fields-Carré Collection)

On the road from Arretium (Arezzo) to Perusia (Perugia) Hannibal had 'trailed his coat' before the consul Caius Flaminius, who commanded a standard consular army of about 25,000 men, before disappearing into a narrow defile north of Lake Trasimene. The arena itself was a natural amphitheatre bounded on all sides by hills or water, a perfect killing ground for an unsuspecting foe. This certainly fits well with the description given by Polybios of 'a narrow and level valley enclosed on both sides by an unbroken line of lofty hills. At the western end of this defile rose a steep eminence with sheer slopes that were difficult to climb; at the western end lay the lake, from which the only access to the valley was a narrow passage which ran along the foot of the hillside' (3.83.1).

Hannibal set his stage with care. He placed his Libyan and Iberian veterans on the ridge blocking the exit from the killing ground, where they would be in plain view of the advancing Romans. His lightly armed troops, with the Gaulish cavalry, were hidden from view behind the crest of the hills on his left, the Gaulish warriors similarly hidden in folds in the ground running down to the defile, and his cavalry, Iberians in the main, and Numidian cavalry near the entrance where they could block it off once the Romans had passed through (Polybios 3.83.2–4). Dispositions made, the army settled down for the night.

Steel shield of the tournament-loving Henri II of France (r. 1547–59), embossed and damascened with silver and gold and attributed to the Parisian goldsmith Etienne Delaube. The embossed scene at the centre of the shield illustrates Hannibal's stunning victory at Cannae, a metaphor for France fighting against the armies of the Holy Roman Empire. (Fordmadoxfraud)

At dawn Caius Flaminius set out after his apparent prey, in thick mist rising from the lake and marshy vegetation, with no apparent attempt at reconnaissance (Polybios 3.84.1). On seeing the Libyan and Iberian outposts the doomed Roman army began to form up for the attack, only to be completely surprised by the rest of the Punic army charging downhill out of the clinging white veil into their flanks and rear. The ambushers had the smell of victory in their nostrils, and once fighting men begin to smell victory they are unbeatable. Unable to organize any effective resistance, most of the Romans were cut down while they were still in marching order, some, undoubtedly scared witless, even drowning in the quiet waters of the lake as they tried to flee. Here too, in this dead-end alley, the consul was slain, by 'a band of Celts' according to Polybios (3.84.6), and by a lone horse warrior of the Insubres named Ducarius according to Livy (22.6.1–4), who recognized Flaminius as the man responsible for the earlier defeat of his people (223 BC). The vanguard, some 6,000 strong, cut its way out, only to be surrounded and captured the following day.

Polybios says (3.84.7) that 15,000 Romans died in that misty defile, but this was probably the total of all who were killed, as Livy (22.7.2), citing the contemporary account of Quintus Fabius Pictor, makes clear, and Polybios' total of 15,000 prisoners (3.85.2) is probably also too high. No matter. The crucial element was Hannibal's disproportionate losses: some 1,500 in all. According to Polybios (3.85.5) most of them were Celts, while Livy (22.7.3) gives the higher figure of 2,500 killed in action with many more later dying of their wounds.

Cannae, August 216 BC

The town of Cannae, Apulia, lay on the right bank of the Aufidus some 8km from the Adriatic Sea, the hill upon which it sat being the last spur of generally rising ground in that direction. Below Cannae the river runs through mainly flat, treeless country, but that on the left bank is noticeably more so than that on the right. The left bank, in fact, is perfect cavalry country, never exceeding a 20m contour throughout the whole area between the town and the sea, whereas on the right bank, though the ground is mostly level, it rises slowly but steadily from the sea to reach the ridge by

Battle of Cannae, August 216 BC

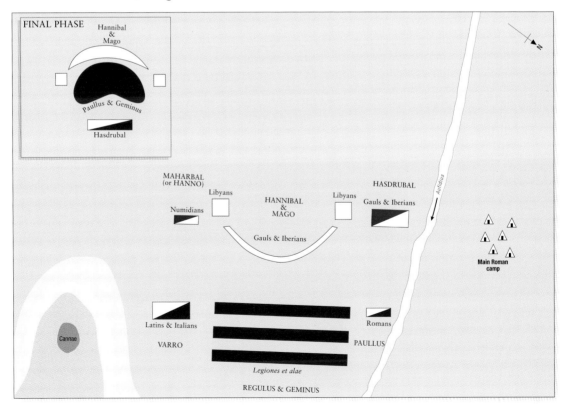

Cannae. However, although some authorities have placed the battle on the left bank (e.g. Dodge 2002: 47–8), it is an easier reading of our best sources to locate the fighting on the right bank, assuming the river's course originally lay farther away from the hill of Cannae itself (e.g. Lazenby 1978: 77–79).

As for the size of the Roman army, Livy (22.36.2–4) reports that it was made up of eight reinforced legions, each of 5,000 infantry and 300 cavalry (instead of the usual 4,000 and 200 respectively), supported by an equal number of Latin-Italian *alae*, each of 5,000 infantry and 600 cavalry. Thus, by Livy's reckoning, there would have been 80,000 infantry and 7,200 cavalry at Cannae. According to Polybios (3.113.5, 117.8), there were 80,000 infantry, 10,000 of whom served as the garrison of the main camp, perhaps one legion and its corresponding Latin-Italian *ala*, and more than 6,000 cavalry. Like Livy, Polybios says (3.107.9–15, cf. 6.20.6–7) the army was organized into eight legions and eight *alae*, each of 5,000 infantry supported by 300 and 900 cavalry respectively. Appian (*Hannibalica* 17) and Plutarch (*Fabius Maximus* 14.2) support these figures, the former claiming that there were 70,000 infantry and 6,000 cavalry excluding camp garrisons, while the latter notes that the combined force amounted to 88,000 men.

The Roman legions, supported by the Latin-Italian *alae*, were drawn up in their customary three lines behind a forward screen of skirmishers. However, not only were the maniples deployed closer together than usual but their frontage was reduced and their depth increased (Polybios 3.113.3). The Roman tactics were to try and smash through the Punic line by sheer weight of numbers as had happened at the Trebbia (Polybios 3.74.3). With this reversion to the principle of sheer mass, the flexibility and manoeuvrability of the manipular legion was renounced and the rigidity of the hoplite phalanx was reinstated. Today, looking back on what was to unfold that fateful day, it is difficult to imagine why the Roman command chose this battle plan; but they did, and there Hannibal outgeneralled them.

Commanding the centre was Marcus Atilius Regulus, the *consul suffectus* of 217 BC, and Cnaeus Servilius Geminus, Flaminius' original colleague (Polybios

3.114.6, cf. Livy 22.40.6). The 2,400-strong citizen cavalry was stationed on the right flank by the Aufidus and commanded by the consul Lucius Aemilius Paullus, whilst his colleague Caius Terentius Varro, who was apparently exercising supreme command for the entire army for the day (Polybios 3.110.4, 113.1, cf. Appian *Hannibalica* 19), took charge of the left with the 3,600-strong Latin-Italian cavalry.

Hannibal commanded on that day roughly 40,000 infantry – Libyans, Iberians and Gauls – and 10,000 cavalry – Iberians, Numidians and Gauls (Polybios 3.114.6). The Punic centre formed up in a single convex line, also screened to its front by skirmishers, composed of the Gaulish and Iberian war bands (Polybios 3.113.8–9). Hannibal himself, with his brother Mago, took up position here. The Libyan veterans, divided into roughly two equal phalanxes – the hoplite rather than the Macedonian version (Polybios 1.33.6, 34.6) – were deployed on the flanks of this thin, crescent-shaped line. However, now dressed and armed with equipment stripped from the dead of the battles of the Trebbia and Lake Trasimene, they looked for the entire world

Marble statue of Hannibal (Paris, musée du Louvre, inv. MR 2093) by Sébastien Slodtz and François Girardon (1704). He is portrayed counting gold rings. After Cannae Hannibal would gather in a bushel the rings torn from the lifeless fingers of more than fivescore consuls, ex-consuls, praetors, aediles, quaestors, military tribunes and scores of the equestrian order (Livy 22.49.16, 23.12.1–2). In other words, most of Rome's military leadership lay on the battlefield. (Fields-Carré Collection)

like Roman legionaries (Polybios 3.87.3, 114.1, Livy 22.46.4). Hannibal's Gaulish and Iberian cavalry, probably 6,500 strong and led by Hasdrubal (one of Hannibal's most senior lieutenants), was stationed on his left wing by the Aufidus, and the Numidians were stationed on his right, led by either Hanno son of Bomilcar (Polybios 3.114.7), who may have been Hannibal's nephew, or Maharbal son of Himilco (Livy 22.46.7, 51.2).

Hannibal launched the Gaulish and Iberian cavalry head-on – the last were certainly trained and equipped to fight en masse (Polybios 3.65.6) – thereby routing the heavily outnumbered citizen cavalry. Instead of being dissipated in useless pursuit, the victors cut behind the advancing Roman juggernaut to fall on the rear of the Latin-Italian cavalry, who had been held in play by the skirmishing Numidian cavalry. The legionaries gradually pushed back the Gaulish and Iberian war bands, but avoided the Libyans, who, like some frightful masquerade, swung inwards to attack the flanks. The Gaulish and Iberian cavalry left the Numidians to pursue the now fleeing Latin-Italian cavalry, and fell on the rear of the legionaries, thus drawing pressure off the Gaulish and Iberian warriors and effectively surrounding the Roman centre.

This, the final phase of the battle, was not to be an affair of tactical sophistication, but of prolonged butchery, a case of kill, kill, kill until nothing moved. The eventual outcome was a massacre and, in Livy's dramatic rhetoric, the carnage was 'a shocking spectacle even to an enemy's eyes' (22.51.5). But we must be doubly cautious while studying the past, it being a mistake to impose the value system of our time upon another. As H. G. Wells wrote, if you make men sufficiently fearful or angry the hot red eyes of cavemen will glare out at you. In the space of a single day some 48,200 Romans were killed (Livy 22.49.15, cf. Polybios 3.117.2–4), while a further 4,500 were rounded up on the battlefield itself (Livy 22.49.18), with 14,200 taken elsewhere (Livy 22.49.13, 50.11, 52.4, cf. Polybios 3.117.7–11). One proconsul, (namely Servilius), two quaestors, 29 military tribunes, 80 senators and a

Genius at work: Hannibal at Cannae

Onasander once reasoned that 'the general must inspire cheerfulness in the army, more by the strategy of his facial expressions than by words; for many distrust speeches on the ground that they have been concocted for the occasion' (*Stratêgikos* 13.3). True, commanders must be upbeat and reasoned optimists. It is clear that Hannibal could be a cheerful card. When looking at the Roman behemoth preparing for the approaching struggle, one of his senior officers, Gisgo, commented nervously on the number of the enemy. Hannibal turned to him with a grave look on his face and replied: 'There is another thing you have not noticed, Gisgo, which is even more amazing – that in all this enormous host opposite there is not one among them called Gisgo' (Plutarch *Fabius Maximus* 15.2–3). The entire staff broke into laughter, and their hilarity rippled through the ranks. There are no hopeless situations, only hopeless men. The Carthaginian David then squared up to the Roman Goliath. The slow descent into one of the most tragic episodes in the annals of Roman military history had begun.

Alongside Hannibal is Mago, who had led the decisive end-of-battle ambush at the Trebbia, and it would be the two brothers who would remain with the Celts and Iberians in the crucial centre that day. Obviously Hannibal's physical presence there would inspire these men to fulfil their difficult task – to back-pedal steadily in the face of the Roman juggernaut without losing their nerve, which could cause them to turn tail. 'Civilized' soldiers would follow their leaders into near-certain death, something 'barbarian' warriors would never do, the first obeying their leaders, while the second do not. Discipline – and 'civilization' – was what made a real army. According to Polybios (3.116.3–4), Hannibal took an active part in the fighting as well as exhorting those around him, thereby embracing the time-honoured advice to all commanders: never send your men to do something you would not do yourself. Moreover, in this particular instance, his example would hopefully suffice to keep the Celts and Iberians from scampering. It was a test of nerves, will and skill.

Describing Hannibal, Livy noted that his 'dress was in no way superior to that of his fellows, but his arms and horses were conspicuous' (21.4.8). Hannibal's war gear was obviously first rate – we are assuming he was on foot this portentous day – but he did not advertise his identity through wearing unnecessarily ostentatious apparel. Unlike Alexander in a helmet shaped like a lion's head, or Caesar with a scarlet cloak, the modest Hannibal did not dress and act in such a way that would make him stand out from the crowd. There was one noticeable thing, however: his left eye appeared to be open wider, expressionless and sightless.

number of ex-consuls, praetors and aediles also perished with the army (Livy 22.49.16). Of the consuls, Aemilius Paullus was killed and Varro fled from the field (Polybios 3.116.12, 16). Of the Carthaginians, some 8,000 'of his [Hannibal's] bravest men' (Livy 22.52.6, cf. Polybios 3.117.6) were killed.

Zama, October 202 BC

The Romans were naturally horrified when the news reached them of the defeat at Cannae and its scale. Of the two consuls, one had fled from the ghastly field, and the other lay rotting upon it, along with those of the preceding

Military historians regard Cannae as a classic example of a successful double-envelopment manoeuvre. On this hot, dusty, treeless plain, as his weak centre back-pedalled and strong wings stood firm, Hannibal annihilated some 50,000 Romans after they were lured forward into the jaws of the Punic army. It was pure Hannibal. This is an aerial view of Cannae (Monte di Canne), looking north-east towards the site of the battle. The modern course of the Aufidus (Ofanto), looping here where it coiled there, can be seen at the top left. (Fields-Carré Collection)

year. First reports made no mention of survivors, and the Senate was told that the entire army had been simply surrounded and exterminated. On that day the Roman army, the largest ever fielded by the Republic, suffered the highest casualty totals in its history; on that day a citizen army, and the society that had created it, were introduced to the full terrors of annihilation. Not until 14 years later, when Roman troops were in Africa, was Rome to exact its revenge for this absolute catastrophe. Having invaded Africa, the brilliant young Scipio turned the tables and Hannibal, the invader of Italy and for 16 years the undefeated antagonist of Rome, was decisively defeated near the small town of Zama. No battle of Hannibal's war had a more definite outcome, and it effectively sealed the fate of his city. Without the resources or willpower to continue the struggle, Carthage sued for peace and the hot war was over.

According to Livy the survivors of Cannae, after serving for several months in Campania, were transported to Sicily where they made up two legions – the *legiones Cannenses*. Later reinforced by the fleet-of-foot survivors of Herdonea (212 BC), all these disgraced legionaries were not to be released from service and were forbidden to return to Italy until the war was over. Ironically, as Livy remarks, these penal-soldiers became the most experienced men in the entire Roman Army, and Scipio saw fit to formally identify their seasoned units as *legio V* and *legio VI*, and make the pair the backbone of his African expeditionary army (204 BC). Livy adds that these were exceptionally strong legions, each of 6,200 legionaries and with the usual complement of citizen cavalry, and then, intriguingly, says: 'Scipio also chose Latin infantry and cavalry from the *Cannensis exercitus* to accompany him' (29.24.13, 14). Obviously, what he calls the *Cannensis exercitus*, the army of Cannae, consisted of survivors, Roman and *socii*, of that slaughterhouse condemned to serve out the war with no prospect of discharge. Scipio, who had likely served with them at Cannae, knew that the day had not really been lost through any cowardice on their part.

The actual size of the invasion force Scipio finally took with him to Africa is difficult to say. Livy mentions (29.25.1–4) three different totals given by unnamed sources, ranging from 10,000 infantry and 2,200 cavalry, through 16,000 infantry and 1,600 cavalry, to a maximum of 35,000 for both arms.

Though he hesitates to opt for the largest figure, it is assumed here that the middle totals represent the number of infantry and cavalry furnished by the *socii*, while the maximum seems most probable for an expedition of this magnitude.

On receiving orders from Carthage to return home, Hannibal, ever faithful to his country, duly abandoned Italy, taking with him those men who wished to leave; we have no record in the ancient sources of their number, but we suspect that it does not seem to have been a very considerable force. We know that before he left Hannibal put on record what he and his army had achieved since setting out from Iberia to confound the majesty of Rome well-nigh 16 years ago. The record, written in Punic and in Greek, the international language of Hannibal's day, was set up at the temple of Hera Lacinia on the cliff edge of the Lacinian promontory 12km south of Kroton, his final headquarters. A generation later the inscription was seen and read by Polybios (3.56.4, cf. 2.24.17, 3.33.18, Livy 21.38.2, 28.46.16, 30.20.6), who took from it the figures for the strength of Hannibal's army when it first entered Italy – 20,000 infantry (12,000 Libyans, 8,000 Iberian) and 6,000 cavalry. There is no mention of elephants, the thing Hannibal's march is remembered for today, but Appian says (*Hannibalica* 1.4) that he set out with 37, and Polybios (3.42.10) has the same number being rafted across the Rhône, but unfortunately no source records how many survived the crossing of the Alps.

Hannibal in Italy, fresco (1503–08) attributed to the Bolognaise painter, Jacopo Ripandi (*fl. c.*1500–16), in the Palazzo dei Conservatori, Rome. Looking very much like a gentleman from the Orient, Hannibal rides an elephant. It is said that when he crossed the great morass that was the Arno Valley, the general himself rode his last surviving elephant. (Fields-Carré Collection)

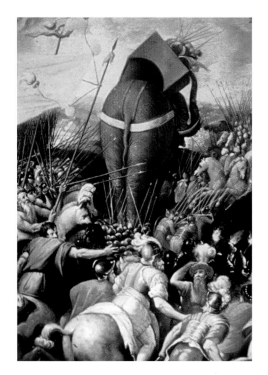

This 16th-century work (Moscow, Pushkin Museum of Fine Arts), attributed to Giulio Romano (1492–1546), presents a rather whimsical version of Zama. The battle itself, which turned out to be the last of the Hannibalic war, must have been grim business, since, as Polybios points out (15.14.6), the antagonists were equal in spirit and courage. (Fields-Carré Collection)

Hannibal landed in the neighbourhood of Hadrumentum 120km south of Carthage, and from here he marched his army to a place Polybios calls Zama, 'a town which lies about five days' march to the west [i.e. south-west] of Carthage' (15.5.3, summarized by Livy 30.29.2). Of the two, three, if not four, places called Zama in the hinterland of ancient Tunisia, the one referred to here has been identified as the one that lay at present-day Seba Biar, some 13km east of Zanfour (Scullard 1970: 142–55, Walbank 1970: 445–51, Lazenby 1978: 218, Lancel 1999: 173–4, Hoyos 2008: 107–8). In keeping with his view of the importance of Zama in shaping the course of world history, Polybios says, with a rare emotional flash, that 'the Carthaginians were fighting for their very survival and the possession of Africa, the Romans for the empire and the sovereignty of the world' (15.9.2). Thus the stage was set for an epic tale.

On the day, Hannibal probably commanded some 36,000 infantry, supported by 4,000 cavalry, half of them valuable Numidian horsemen, and 80 elephants (Polybios 15.3.6, 11.1, 14.9). Appian (*Bellum Punicum* 41) gives Scipio 23,000 Roman and Latin-Italian infantry and 1,500 cavalry. His infantry included those two penal legions, the *legiones Cannenses* now numbered as *legio V* and *legio VI*. Masinissa, a Numidian prince of great ability who had once fought for Carthage, brought with him a force of 6,000 infantry and 4,000 cavalry (Polybios 15.5.12, Livy 30.29.4). Hannibal was perhaps stronger in total, but weaker in cavalry.

Hannibal was therefore in the unaccustomed position of having to rely on his infantry to provide the decisive impact, and these he deployed in three lines, which was the standard formation for the Romans but unusual for the Carthaginians. The first line was composed of Ligurians, Gauls, Balearic slingers and some Moors, presumably lightly armed warriors fighting with javelins, and appears to be the remnants of his brother's mercenaries brought back from Liguria. These were at any rate professionals and therefore troops of reasonable worth, and Polybios says (15.11.1) that there were 12,000 of them in this line, their flanks being covered by the cavalry; the Carthaginians (Punic, Libyphoenician) were to the right and the Numidians to the left, with the elephants and skirmishers screening their front. The second line consisted of Punic, Libyphoenician and Libyan levies hastily raised for the defence of Africa, and probably therefore with little preliminary training or previous experience.

The third line, some distance behind the others and in reserve, consisted of Hannibal's own veterans, that is, the soldiers who had come with him from Italy (Polybios 15.11.2). Though Livy (30.33.6) makes these men Italians, predominantly Bruttians, they must have included all the survivors

Battle of Zama, 202 BC

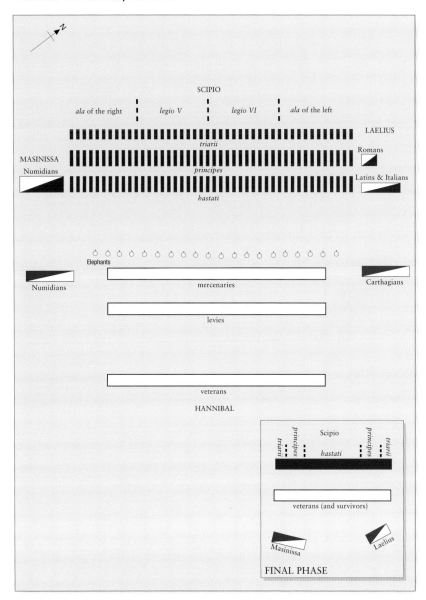

of his Italian army, even some Libyans and Iberians who had marched with him from Iberia and the Gauls who had joined him in Gallia Cisalpina. Livy has blundered badly here because Polybios says (15.11.7–9) that Hannibal, in a pre-battle address, told these grizzled and lean men to remember above all the victories they had gained over the Romans at the Trebbia, Lake Trasimene and Cannae, and later Polybios emphasizes that they were 'the most warlike and the steadiest of his fighting troops' (15.16.4). Livy, believing Hannibal's third line was composed of unenthusiastic Italians, has him place them there 'since their doubtful loyalty might prove them either friend or foe' (30.35.9). Frontinus too says these men were 'Italians, whose loyalty he [Hannibal] distrusted and whose indifference he feared, inasmuch as he had dragged most of them from Italy against their will' (*Strategemata* 2.3.16). Frontinus, in all likelihood, has used Livy as his source here. It seems safest to follow Polybios' account.

What would the military connoisseur have made of Hannibal's army and his state of affairs? For the first time in his career, the Carthaginian general was fighting on ground not of his choosing. Up to now Hannibal had always made the terrain fight for him, choosing his battlefields with great care and refusing battle until the ground suited him. Moreover, the sharp-eyed observer could hardly fail to notice that Hannibal was also fighting with inferiority in the mounted arm, which had always played a large and decisive part in all his victories. As Polybios himself once explained, 'the cavalry was the arm on which he [Hannibal] relied above all others' (3.101.8). What is more, not only was he rather deficient in this particular, but most of what he had was not of much use.

Scipio had no such worries in this particular department. For it was during his campaign in Iberia that he had struck up a friendship with Masinissa, and now on African soil his brilliant horsemen would prove crucial allies. Scipio stationed the prince and his Numidians on the right wing, and his friend and right-hand man, Caius Laelius, with the citizen and Latin-Italian cavalry on the left wing. In the centre the Roman and Latin-Italian legionaries were drawn up in the standard *triplex acies*, except that the maniples of *hastati*, *principes* and *triarii*, instead of deployed chequer-wise, were placed one behind the other leaving clear lanes to accommodate the elephants. All his *velites* were stationed in these lanes with orders to fall back in front of the beasts to the rear of the whole formation, or, if that proved difficult, to turn right and left between the lines, leaving the lanes clear for the elephants (Polybios 15.9.7–10).

In the event, a large proportion of the elephants, being young and untrained, were frightened out to the wings where they did more harm to their own side than to Scipio's, thereby helping his cavalry to sweep their counterparts from the field (Polybios 15.12.2–5). For Hannibal's elephants and cavalry the battle of Zama was over.

It was now time for the main business to commence, and the opposing first lines (the *hastati* and the mercenaries) clashed and set to. In Livy's patriotic account the Romans sweep all before them (30.34.3), but Polybios more soberly says that at first the mercenaries, who were professionals after all, prevailed through their 'courage and skill' (15.13.1). It was indeed a soldier's battle, with each man fighting for his own hand, a life-and-death struggle in a most brutal sense. Once the *hastati*, now probably reinforced by some of the *principes*, had eventually broken and scattered the second Carthaginian line, it too by all accounts having put up a desperate display of doggedness, Scipio redeployed his second and third lines on either wing of the first. If, as on previous occasions, Scipio planned to outflank the Carthaginian third line with his *principes* and *triarii*, this was not to be.

Tactical readjustments made, Scipio then closed with Hannibal's veterans, who were also probably now flanked by a substantial number of survivors from their first two lines, Polybios indicating that the two forces were nearly equal in numbers. The veterans of both sides were now pitched eyeball to eyeball, and the nerves of Scipio and Hannibal were to be tested to the utmost. Up to this point of the battle, Scipio must have been acutely aware that Hannibal had never yet been defeated, but from the moment the citizen-allied and Numidian cavalry returned and fell on Hannibal's rear, his cause was lost (Polybios 15.14.6). The surviving mercenaries and levies turned and fled; Hannibal escaped with a scanty band of horsemen, but his hard-nosed veterans, largely armed and equipped in the Roman style, if they did have such an option they despised it. They fought bitterly to the death, pitted against those very legionaries that they had disgraced at Cannae. The military connoisseur can use a little licence to fill in the final, tragic details, enabling us to envisage not so much as a single man asking quarter or throwing down his arms, but each fighting without holding back and defending himself to the finish.

Polybios concludes his account of the battle with the view that Hannibal had done all that a good general of long experience should have done, 'brave man as he was, he met another better' (15.16.6, quoting *Iliad* 4.300), and left the tattered remains of his veterans to their self-elected doom. It seems that on the field of Zama, much like Napoleon on that of Waterloo, Hannibal could not avoid defeat. Unlike his brother Hasdrubal, who in similar circumstances had died with sword in hand, Hannibal took the longer view. Very probably he would have preferred to exit alongside his faithful veterans, to die like Leonidas, but quite sensibly thought of Carthage first: alive, he could still hope to have some influence on events and continue to serve his country in peace as he had in war.

The less charitable view is that he lost his nerve and abandoned the field of disaster in fear of being taken by his enemies and bundled off to Rome

The route followed by Hannibal from Emporion in Iberia to Illiberis (Elne) in Gaul is not precisely known, but he presumably traversed the Pyrenees somewhere at their eastern extremity. Having left a sizeable force to hold the newly conquered territory, he crossed the mountains with an army of about 50,000 infantry and 9,000 cavalry (Polybios 3.35.7). This is a general view of Banyuls-sur-mer, France, with the Pyrenees behind. Hannibal may have crossed this mountain chain via the col de Banyuls (361m) nearby. (Rodolphe Naudi)

(the recent fate of the Numidian king Syphax). True, he could have stayed in a glorious attempt to rally the survivors, but his army had virtually ceased to exist: Polybios assesses the Carthaginian casualties as being 20,000 dead and 20,000 prisoners, figures repeated by Livy but not by Appian, who gives 25,000 dead and only 8,500 prisoners. Whichever is correct it demonstrates the ferocity of the fighting and the completeness of Hannibal's defeat. As to the Roman losses, Polybios' number of no more than 1,500 killed seems ridiculously low. Appian, however, assesses the Roman losses at 2,500 and those of Masinissa still more (Polybios 15.14.9, Livy 30.35.3, Appian *Bellum Punicum* 48).

Two minds meet: Hannibal at Zama

In the spring of 204 BC, Scipio took an army composed of volunteers and veterans of Rome's humiliations at Cannae and Herdonea to Africa. The following spring he was victorious over a Punic army at the Great Plains, and Carthage sued for peace. Hannibal then returned from Italy and hostilities were soon renewed. By the autumn of 202 BC the time had come for Hannibal to meet his Roman doppelgänger, Scipio, on the field of Zama. Between the two camps the two commanders met for their famous parley (Polybios 15.6–8 *passim*, Livy 30.29.1–10, cf. Frontinus *Strategemata* 1.1.3, 6.2.1, 2), each with an interpreter although both spoke Greek, and Hannibal perhaps Latin (cf. Livy 22.13.6, Zonaras 8.24). On the opening page of his great work Clausewitz makes a very simple yet very profound statement, 'War is nothing but a duel on a large scale' (*Vom Krieg* 1.1.2), and he likens it to a bout between two wrestlers. For their meeting our two men of violence have come dressed for war.

Scipio wears an Etrusco-Corinthian style of helmet with a horsehair crest, and a short, decorated and muscled cuirass of bronze. The latter has two rows of *pteruges* of white linen with gilded fringes, and is bound round with a specially tied linen waistband. Underneath is a tunic of fine white wool edged with purple (to denote senatorial rank). Over the top he has thrown a long woollen cloak, which is coloured scarlet, as are his crest and waistband. He has snap-on bronze greaves and sandal-type boots, called *caligae*. On his left hip hangs an Iberian cut-and-thrust sword, a straight-bladed, sharp-pointed weapon from which the Roman *gladius* would evolve.

Hannibal too carries an Iberian straight sword, but the similarities end there. He wears a simple iron plate corselet, unadorned Attic helmet, also of iron, well-worn Greek-style boots and a dun-coloured, coarse woollen cloak. We see him with a short, neatly trimmed, thick beard and moustache, the face of a mature man with much experience of life behind him. His good eye has become a narrow slit, a result of constant squinting into the blazing sun of southern Italy. He is trim and fit, as always – no middle-age bulge for the 45-year-old Hannibal.

Scipio's interpreter wears a belted linen tunic, bleached white, broad and full, and gathered at the waist to hang just below the knees. Over this he has put a heavy woollen cloak, dyed yellow-brown, fastened at the right shoulder by means of a silver circular brooch and reaching to the calves.

Hannibal's interpreter wears a Carthaginian-style tunic, which is knee-length, loose and full, with long sleeves. Over this he has thrown a Gaulish-style cloak, of heavyweight wool, rectangular in shape, without sleeves or hood, gaudy and brooch-fastened. Both men are unarmed.

Graeco-Roman theatre, Ephesos, looking east-north-east from 'St Paul's Prison'. It was here, according to Cicero, that Hannibal was invited to attend a lecture by one Phormio, and, after being treated to a lengthy discourse on the art of generalship, was asked by his friends what he thought of it. 'I have seen many old drivellers', he replied, 'on more than one occasion, but I have seen no one who drivelled more than Phormio' (*de oratore* 2.18.75). It was also at Ephesos, or so say Livy and Plutarch, that Hannibal met his old adversary, Scipio. They apparently discussed world-famous generals. (Fields-Carré Collection)

This battle ended Hannibal's war, but Hannibal himself would continue to cast a long shadow in the dimming light of recent events. He lived 19 years after the battle of Zama, the last he ever fought, and the first he ever lost. Rome never felt safe until his death.

The way of the general

There is a famous injunction of the Chinese master strategist, Sun Tzu, that goes: 'Knowing the other and knowing oneself / In one hundred battles no danger' (3.31 Denma Translation). Polybios agrees, saying that 'there is no more precious asset for a general than knowledge of his opponent's guiding principles and character… The commander must train his eye upon the weak spots of his opponent's defence, not in his body but in his mind' (3.81.1,3). Shrewdness was a quality, says Polybios (2.36.3), which led to Hannibal's appointment as the leader of the Punic forces in Iberia.

Fighting his first pitched battle on Italian soil in bitter winter conditions along the Trebbia, Hannibal had cleverly used seemingly flat and open country to mask an ambuscade. The Romans, having emerged from their tents on empty stomachs and waded across the swollen river that snowy, solstice forenoon, lost two-thirds of their half-starved and rheumatic army before nightfall. It is said that fortune is fond of crafty men, but she also smiles upon those who thoroughly prepare themselves for her gift of victory. That morning Hannibal had ordered his men to enjoy a hearty breakfast (a commander must think about his soldiers' stomachs) and to rub their bodies with olive oil around their campfires (Polybios 3.71.6). The balance of fortune tipped in favour of the Punic invader.

For military historians, the battle of the Trebbia suitably illustrates the many facets of Hannibal's military genius. Here they can witness his psychological insight into the minds of his Roman opponents, his concern for the welfare of his own men, his willingness to try the unexpected, and his ability to use each element in his army to the best advantage within the parameters of a simple battle plan. It is also the only pitched battle, apart from Zama, in which he used elephants. Tactically, it demonstrates Hannibal's principle of double envelopment, albeit with the extra refinement of an ambush. After the usual preliminary skirmishing, Hannibal's infantry pinned the Roman infantry in place while his cavalry drove back the Roman cavalry from the wings, exposing the flanks of the Roman infantry and allowing the Numidian horsemen and Punic lightly armed troops to harass them. As if on cue, the ambush force launched themselves on the Roman rear.

Hannibal was a great exponent of ambush, and Lake Trasimene, his next engagement, was to be based on one giant snare rather than a formal head-to-head battle. Marching along the northern shore of the lake, Hannibal very visibly pitched camp at the eastern end of the line of hills

Pont Saint-Bénezet, Palace of the Popes, Avignon. Hannibal crossed the broad river Rhône somewhere in the vicinity of Avignon, ferrying his 37 elephants across on camouflaged rafts. Several hypotheses exist, but Napoleon (*Commentaires*, vol. VI, p. 159) was probably correct in setting the limits between the Rhône's tributaries, the Durance and the Ardèche. (Günter Wieschendahl)

that ran parallel to, and overhung, the lakeside. During the night he divided his troops into several columns and led them round behind the same hills, taking up positions parallel with the path the army had traversed earlier that day. Most, if not all, of the troops were positioned on the reverse slopes of the high ground, concealed from the enemy's view when the sun came up. As the first glimmerings of opalescent dawn dissolved the darkness, Flaminius hurried his men on with the expectation of closing with his quarry. The morning was misty, the line of hills mostly obscured by a clinging white veil, but it is possible that the straining eyes of Flaminius could just glimpse the Carthaginian camp at the far end of the narrow defile. While the consul sat upon his finely accoutred horse and dreamed of martial glory, those further down the pecking order shambled through the morning mire and dreamed mostly of more mundane things. Fate seeks no man's head – each man's head goes to meet its fate.

   As has been pointed out, Polybios saw that the most important quality for a general was the ability to understand the character and methods of his opponent, since moral and psychological flaws lead to weaknesses that can be turned to an advantage. Thus it was knowledge of Flaminius' self-confidence, says Polybios (3.80.3), which enabled Hannibal to lure him into his lakeside ambuscade. Doubtless too, Hannibal had counted on the early morning mist to rise over the lake and it's miry margins – it was around the time of the summer solstice – and from the moment that his trap was sprung his victory was certain. The Roman soldiers could see little, since the heavy mist from the lake still blanketed the defile and visibility was limited. Instead they heard outlandish war cries and the clash of weapons from many different directions simultaneously. In a world of mistaken shadows and magnified sounds, the mist-blinded consular army was soon thrown into utter confusion. 'In the chaos that reigned,' records Livy, 'not a soldier could recognize his own standard or knew his place in the ranks – indeed, they were almost too bemused to get proper control over their swords and shields, while to some their very armour and weapons proved not a defence but fatal

Hannibal was singularly agile at guessing what his enemy would do, and could act on it with speed and effect. This is a marble head of Alexander (Pélla, Museum of Archaeology, inv. GL 15), in a near-contemporary portrayal. (Fields-Carré Collection)

For what Polybios calls 'the ascent towards the Alps' (3.50.1), there are two main contenders for the honour of having been Hannibal's route from the basin of the Rhône to the watershed pass. By marching up the valley of the Isère in the north he may have used an 'Isère Pass', namely Col du Petit Saint-Bernard (2,188m), Col du Mont-Cenis (2,083m) or Col de Clapier (2,482m). This is a panoramic view of the Isère Valley from the Massif de la Chartreuse. (Author's collection)

encumbrance' (22.5.5). By the time the sun was high enough to burn off the last wisps of mist, some 15,000 men had perished in battle (if that is what it can be called) and the consul himself had fallen heroically, dispatched by a Gaulish spear. So much for Flaminius.

Hannibal was a genius, not a mere general, and unsurprisingly his genius has seldom been questioned. It rested on a mixture of bluff and double bluff, and a truly remarkable ability to use all types of troops to their best advantage. This he did by a combination of flexible tactics and pushing the native skills of his troops to the limits of their ability. Ardent du Picq (1946: 76) writes:

> Hannibal was the greatest general of antiquity by reason of his admirable comprehension of morale of combat, of the morale of the soldier whether his own or the enemy's. He shows his greatest in this respect in all the different incidents of war, of campaign, of action. His men were not better than the Roman soldiers. They were not as well armed, one-half less in number. Yet he was always the conqueror. He understood the value of morale. He had the absolute confidence of his people. In addition he had the art, in commanding an army, of always securing the advantage of morale.

His third battle, Cannae, remains a *chef-d'oeuvre* to which generations of subsequent generals have aspired. Roman strength lay in the set-piece battle, the decisive clash of opposing armies that settled the issue one way or another. In its crudest form, the two sides would deploy in close order, slowly advance, clash, and systematically set about butchering one another until one or the other could stand it no longer. And even success was dearly bought. Tellingly, Polybios saw the Romans as rather old-fashioned in their straightforward and open approach to warfare, commenting that as a race they tended to rely instinctively on 'brute force' (*bía*, 1.37.7) when making war.

Nothing illustrates his criticism better than the battle of Cannae, when Roman tactics subordinated the other arms very much to the heavy infantry, who were to carry the heat and burden of that terrible day. Indeed, there was all the delirium of amateur soldiering (we are still in a world of seasonal campaigns and militia armies) in them that midsummer morning as they ponderously rolled forward at a moderate rate in open terrain, their ranks unusually packed into a close and solid mass, a veritable steamroller in motion. And on they tramped with heads up, moving ever forward in a courageous manner, but courage does not always win battles and it was not to do so in this case. Hannibal was about to demonstrate to the Romans that there was more to the art of war than mere brute force.

Being faced by a vastly more numerous army, Hannibal decided, in effect, to use the very strength of the enemy infantry to defeat it, deliberately inviting it to press home its attack on the centre of his line. According to plan, his now Roman-equipped Libyans would serve as the two jaws of this primitive trap, the Gauls and Iberians as the bait. Finally, Hannibal took equal care with the deployment of his cavalry; it too would play an integral part in the entrapment of the Romans. All too often, swept up in the hot pursuit of routing opponents, victorious cavalry disappeared from the actual field of battle, leaving their infantry comrades to battle on alone. Hannibal, keeping in mind that cavalry in a charge do not have to kill to get the job done, anticipated his to do otherwise. And so instead of distributing his cavalry equally between the wings, he would place more on the left against the river. This virtually guaranteed a breakthrough against the numerically far-inferior citizen cavalry, and it would then be available for further manoeuvres on the battleground. The smaller body of cavalry on the open flank, away from the river, where the more numerous Latin-Italian cavalry was stationed, would be expected to hold them in play for as long as possible. As mentioned before, Hannibal's use of cavalry was not done in imitation of Alexander's tactics, yet the two commanders could not have agreed more in respect of the coordination of arms. The Carthaginian dispositions at Cannae, made in full view of the enemy and on a treeless space, actually constituted an ambush. Not only was this a beautifully thought out and audacious scheme, but it showed Hannibal's absolute confidence in the fighting abilities of all the contingents of his mixed army.

Hannibal may have deployed his army, as was convention in antiquity, with cavalry on the wings, infantry in the centre, and the skirmishers thrown out some distance from the main battle line. However, what he did with his infantry was highly unconventional. His relatively thin centre was bowed

Alternatively, by marching up the middle reaches of the valley of the Durance in the south, Hannibal may have used a 'Durance Pass'. This is a view of the river Durance in the vicinity of Manosque. (Pierre Lavaurs)

Col de Montgenèvre (1,854m), Hautes-Alpes, with the obelisk honouring Napoleon. Edward Gibbon (*Decline & Fall*, vol. I, p. 314, n. 1) had Hannibal go this way. (Author's collection)

Col de Larche (1,991m), sometimes Col de l'Argentière, Alpes-de-Haute-Provence. This is the watershed pass François I crossed, in June 1515, with cavalry, infantry, artillery and baggage train en route to his bloody victory over the Swiss at Marignano (now known as Melignano), on the Milan–Lodi road. (Twice25)

out towards the Romans – Polybios' terminology is precise, calling this extraordinary formation a *mênoeides kurtôma*, or 'a crescent-moon-shaped convexity' (3.113.8) – both to screen the Libyans on the wings and to give the impression that the line was deeper than it actually was. But the real beauty of its shape was in the fact that it gave a greater distance for the retreat and bought more time: the longer the bait back-pedalled without breakdown, the easier the waiting jaws might enclose the obliging Romans. Sheer panic would then do the rest. Colonel Ardent du Picq believed that Hannibal had guessed right that the 'terror' and 'surprise' resulting from his trap would outweigh 'the courage of despair in the masses' (1946: 75). A dense formation many ranks deep was an intimidating sight to behold as it approached, and the close proximity of their comrades all round them encouraged the Romans, who formed the solid mass. Such a formation possessed phenomenal staying power in combat, increasing the chance that the enemy's morale would crack first. Yet in this case it was to no avail, as Hannibal had the measure of his fellow man, and in man there is by nature a strong herd instinct.

Before Zama, Hannibal never had known defeat. Yet the more we look at this battle, the more we can appreciate his real genius. Look at his third line, which was not only the best but very much the strongest of the three, and it becomes clear that Hannibal's order of battle represented not a plan of attack but an elaborate plan of defence, by which the Romans were expected to penetrate a succession of screens. The first screen was the elephants, then the missile-throwing troops (Balearic slingers, Moorish javelineers) with a stiffening of men accustomed to fighting at close quarters (Ligurians, Gauls), then close-order infantry (African levies). They then reached the third and final line – Hannibal's 'old guard', if you will – tough and intact. Moreover, this line was kept some way back so survivors from the first two lines had ground enough to rally on. When it came to the crunch, Hannibal believed that his army, with its levies and motley cavalry, could win. Hannibal's conscripts and cavalry were not brilliant, but they were not bad. Polybios' sober judgement on this particular matter (15.16.2–4) says it all:

> He [Hannibal] had massed that large force of elephants and stationed them in front with the express purpose of throwing the enemy into confusion and breaking their ranks. He had also drawn up the mercenaries in front with the Carthaginians [i.e. the levies] behind them in the hope that the enemy would become physically exhausted, and their swords lose their edge through the sheer volume of the carnage before the final engagement took place. Besides this, by keeping the Carthaginians hemmed in on both sides he compelled them to stand fast and fight, so that in Homer's words, 'Even those loth to fight

should be forced to take part in the battle' [*Iliad* 4.300]. Meanwhile, he kept the most warlike and the steadiest of his fighting troops at some distance in the rear. He intended that they should watch the battle from a distance, leaving their strength and their spirit unimpaired until he could draw upon their martial qualities at the critical moment.

In other words, Hannibal expected his veterans to deliver a *coup de grâce* to the badly damaged Romans. The failure of the plan to thin, halt or turn the Roman attack was due entirely to Hannibal's weakness on the two wings, for Scipio by the rapid victory of his cavalry had time to take stock and re-form for the final showdown with the 'old guard', which was soon surrounded by the victorious horsemen returning from their hunt.

Indeed, the return of Scipio's cavalry was decisive, for until it arrived the outcome was doubtful, Polybios saying that 'the contest for a long while hung in the balance until Masinissa and Laelius returned from the pursuit of the Carthaginian cavalry and arrived by a stroke of fortune at the critical moment' (15.14.7). Here Polybios uses the term *daimónios* (literally: 'marvellously [timed]'), but Livy omits the qualifying adjective. Naturally, our Roman historian patriotically overlooks the extreme uncertainty of the final stages of the contest. Whatever else one may say (or think), for Scipio the timing was perfect, and as Napoleon once said: 'The fate of a battle is a question of a single moment, a single thought... the decisive moment arrives, the moral spark is kindled, and the smallest reserve force settles the argument' (*Mémoires*, vol. II, p. 15).

Many qualities are required in a commander. Different pundits have different perspectives about which are the more important. In the opinion of Clausewitz (*Vom Krieg* 1.3, 'On Military Genius'), the virtues of the ideal

Col du Mont-Cenis (2,083m), Savoie, the watershed pass Napoleon thought Hannibal used. On 20 May 1800, the First Consul himself swept over the Alps into Italy, using the Col du Grand Saint-Bernard (2,469m), astride a sturdy mule and wearing a simple grey waistcoat. 'We have fallen like a thunderbolt', he wrote four days later to his brother Joseph (*Correspondance,* vol. VI, no. 4836, p. 308). On 14 June he was to gain a celebrated victory at Marengo, a battle that he should have lost. (Gunther Hissler)

commander can be distilled into three outstanding qualities. The first is that figuratively expressed by the French term *coup d'oeil* (literally: 'a glance'), a quality embracing two attributes: a fairly commonplace knack of judging how many men a given position can contain, a trick that is acquired through practice, and of being able to assess at first sight all the strengths and weaknesses of the terrain. In its broadest sense, *coup d'oeil* is the facility of seeing and doing, both accurately and quickly.

The second quality of the ideal commander is strength of character, by which Clausewitz means 'tenacity of conviction'. In other words, the commander should stick to a plan, once made, 'and not give up until a clear conviction forces him to do so'.

The third, and most important, quality of the ideal commander is resolution. Here, Clausewitz describes, rather than defines, this intangible:

So long as a unit fights cheerfully, with spirit and élan great strength of will is rarely needed; but once conditions become difficult, as they must when much is at stake, things no longer run like a well-oiled machine. The machine itself begins to resist, and the commander needs tremendous will power to overcome this resistance. The machine's resistance need not consist of disobedience and argument, though this occurs often enough in individual soldiers. It is the

Presumed marble portrait bust of Hannibal (Naples, Museo Archeologico Nazionale), found near Naples. Strong suspicions exist that this is actually a Renaissance work and not a Roman portrait, and in fact we have no authentic likeness (unlike Alexander or Caesar) of him. (Fields-Carré Collection)

Napoleon Crossing the Alps, engraving by John Jackson (1778–1831). Obviously inspired by Jacques-Louis David's iconic oil canvas of 1801, a more accurate version would feature Napoleon as a small, huddled, silent, irresistible figure perched on a surefooted mule instead of heroically astride a fiery steed. As for Hannibal himself, he may well have crossed on foot wrapped in pelts. (Ancient Art & Architecture)

Hannibal's descent from the Alps took him into the territory of the Taurini, 'who lived at the foot of the mountains' (Polybios 3.60.8). Mortal enemies of his allies the Insubres, they rejected his advances. In response he stormed their chief settlement – probably the site of Turin – and massacred its inhabitants. This calculated act of terror convinced other neighbouring Celtic tribes to join him. This is a general view of Turin, with the Cottian Alps (France/Italy) in the background. (Author's collection)

impact the ebbing of moral and physical strength, of the heartrending spectacle of the dead and wounded, that the commander has to withstand – first in himself, and then in all those who, directly or indirectly, have entrusted him with their thoughts and feelings, hopes and fears. As each man's strength gives out, as it no longer responds to his will, the inertia of the whole gradually comes to rest on the commander's will alone. The ardour of his spirit must rekindle the flame of purpose in all others; his inward fire must revive their hope.

The ideal commander, then, has to conspicuously display his 'tremendous willpower' at the crisis of battle, thereby lifting his men to that supreme effort that gives final victory. This display is to be distinguished from personal heroism.

Clausewitz's paragon of generalship can certainly be retrospectively applied to Hannibal. But how well did Hannibal live up to Clausewitz's ideals? He certainly had *coup d'oeil*, that quick and sure grasp of time and terrain. Yet as well as being able to take a situation in with a glance and then act with great decisiveness, he also had a tenacious retentiveness and paid close attention to detail, with what he assimilated serving not only his memory, but his mind too. He was a philosopher as well as a commander, an analyser as well as an actor. To illustrate all this, one telling example will suffice.

Old Fabius Maximus did once manage to trap Hannibal in a narrow valley, and for a while the Carthaginian seemed finally to be bottled in. He escaped by tying dry faggots to the horns of the strongest of his camp cattle, which were then driven towards the high ground dominating the pass out of the valley, and the faggots were ignited. All these late-night illuminations fooled the soldiers guarding the pass, who rushed up the hills. Of course, by the time they had discovered their blunder, Hannibal had quietly slipped away in the dark. The following morning he, with his usual care, rescued the soldiers that had been detailed to handle the oxen (Polybios 3.93.1–94.7, Frontinus *Strategemata* 1.5.28).

'A battle avoided cannot be lost', runs one of those ancient Chinese adages, and it seems that Fabius was doing just that. Hardly surprising when we consider his alternative was to commit himself to the lottery of a night action over broken and uneven terrain. And so Fabius predictably did what Hannibal had anticipated: nothing. Hannibal was singularly apt at guessing what his enemy would do, and so knowing the mind of his opposite number his ruse was designed to be recognized as such by Fabius. He was confident too of a shocking psychological truth: contrary to popular belief, people do not learn by experience. Instead, they respond to a particular stimulus in a particular way, and this repeatedly. Again and again this undeviating, compulsive response may be observed, and generation after generation, in accordance with the laws of human behaviour, the dismal message reappears like writing on the wall. Hannibal maintained his ascendancy by the acuteness of his mind and his knowledge of human nature.

Hannibal is rightly praised for his 'marches, tactics, and pitched battles in Italy' (Polybios 7.4.4). Yet when all is said and done, perhaps the clearest light on Hannibal's character is shown by the fact that although he maintained his ragtag mercenary army permanently on active service in what was often hostile territory for almost 16 unbroken years, he kept it 'free from sedition towards him or among themselves... the ability of their commander forced men so radically different to give ear to a single word of command and yield obedience to a single will' (Polybios 11.19.3, 5). If this is how Polybios saw Hannibal, then his inspirational leadership and canny people management must have been unsurpassed. As well as a great strategist he must also have been a great contriver, a practical expert who clearly knew how to compromise in order to accommodate the broad ethnic diversity of the assorted national and tribal contingents that constituted his mixed army of disinterested soldiers.

Success in war comes from a combination of the skill and daring of the commander and the skill and confidence of the commanded. A commander gets a full response from all those under his command only by something approaching a complete fusion of his own identity with the whole that he and they together form. Hannibal's real contribution to the art of generalship was mental, not physical, his presence on a battlefield being decisive not because of his bravery, but because of his brain. To Hannibal, I think, the act of commanding was a cerebral joy.

OPPOSING COMMANDERS

It could be argued that one major disadvantage for Rome was the limited ability of its aristocratic generals, but there is no real proof that the employment of grim professional soldiers in command would have improved matters. Hannibal's obvious skill as a general inflicted this catastrophic defeat on its militia army, yet the same type of army, when better led and with higher morale, beat him in turn at Zama. As Polybios rightly points out, 'the defeats they suffered had nothing to do with weapons or formations, but were brought about by Hannibal's cleverness and military genius' (18.28.7).

It has been said that Alexander had only one worthy opponent, namely Memnon the Rhodian, whereas Hannibal was pitted against many great generals. In truth, Hannibal was pitted against something far greater than one individual. The Roman military system was precisely that, a system. Rome did not need brilliant generals of the type of Alexander or Hannibal, and rarely produced them, it just needed to replicate and reproduce its legions, which it did on an almost industrial basis, though apparently at the phenomenal cost of 10 per cent of its entire male population (Brunt 1971: 28). War is not an intellectual activity but a brutally physical one, and the bloody reality is that all wars are won through fighting and most through attrition, both moral and physical. By an ironic but saving paradox, Romans were at their very best only when in the most straitened circumstances; its enemies knew that all wars with Rome would have a long run because Rome never gave up. Anyway, what follows are brief entries on a few of the major players in Hannibal's career, to indicate the nature of the commanders against whom he had to measure himself.

Caius Flaminius (d. 217 BC)

Caius Flaminius (*cos.* I 223 BC, *censor* 220 BC, *cos.* II 217 BC) was a *novus homo* ('new man'), one of that small number in any generation of Roman politics who were the first in their family to hold Rome's highest

Marble statue of Quintus Fabius Maximus Cunctator at Schloss Schönbrunn, Vienna. Having been severely mauled at the battles of the Trebbia and Lake Trasimene, Rome was saved by Fabius, who adopted the now-famous 'Fabian strategy'. By this campaign of painful delay and devastation, for close to six months the Romans simply refused to take to the field against Hannibal. (Author's collection)

magistracy, the consulship, which was usually dominated by a small group of aristocratic families. Both Polybios (3.80.3–82.8) and Livy (21.63.1–15, 22.3.3–14) portray him as an aggressive demagogue, a man of bold words but little talent who had based his career on pandering to the desires of the poorest citizens.

As for his abilities, while serving as tribune of the people (232 BC) he had succeeded in passing a far-sighted bill to distribute much of the land recently seized near Ariminum (Rimini) to poorer citizens, as a praetor (227 BC) he had been the first governor of Sicily, and as a censor (220 BC) he had overseen the building of the Via Flaminia, the great consular road that ran from Rome to Ariminum and the newly colonized land in the north, and the Circus Flaminius. Moreover, as consul in 223 BC he had commanded in the field in Gallia Cisalpina with considerable success – yet success against northerners was no real preparation for facing a commander of Hannibal's calibre.

Having defeated the Insubres and returned triumphant to Rome, it is interesting to note that the people voted Flaminius a triumph in spite of the opposition of most of the Senate (*Fasti Triumphales* 530 AUC). Even before he kept the deadly rendezvous, Flaminius' career had certainly been controversial, but it had also been exceptionally distinguished, even by the standards of the period, and especially so for a *novus homo*. It seems though that the maverick Flaminius had made many enemies en route, men who saw him as a fool who rode to his death, and would who savage his reputation thereafter.

Quintus Fabius Maximus Cunctator (275–203 BC)

In the wake of the disaster at Lake Trasimene Rome took the traditional remedy of appointing a dictator, a single magistrate with supreme powers, something it had not done for three decades. Quintus Fabius Maximus (*cos*. I 233 BC, *censor* 230 BC, *cos*. II 228 BC, *dict*. 217 BC, *cos*. III 215 BC, *cos*. IV 214 BC, *cos*. V 209 BC) was now 58 years of age, rather old for a Roman general, and had served as a youth in the First Punic War, subsequently being twice elected to the consulship. He was to gain the pejorative cognomen 'Cunctator', the Delayer, because, recognizing that he was not able to cope with Hannibal on the field of battle, he wisely chose to conduct a campaign of delays and limited-scale war, the one thing Hannibal could not afford, but also the one thing the Romans could not tolerate or understand. His officers and soldiers contemptuously called him 'Hannibal's *paedogogus*' after the slave (Greek, invariably) who followed a Roman schoolboy carrying his books (Plutarch *Fabius Maximus* 5.3).

There can be little doubt, by exercising the privilege of hindsight, that at this time Fabius' strategy of caution and delay was the correct one, and that his appointment prevented yet another consular army being served up to meet its almost inevitable doom at Hannibal's hands in 217 BC. As Polybios sagely remarks (3.89.8–9), in refusing to be drawn into pitched battles, Fabius was falling back on factors in which Rome had the advantage, namely inexhaustible supplies of men and *matériel*.

But it was bound to be unpopular and unspectacular, and it was to prove extremely costly to the Italian countryside, particularly in the *ager Falernus*, the spreading plain of Campania with is celebrated vineyards (Polybios 3.90.7–92.10, Livy 22.13.1–15.1). All credit must be given to Fabius for the iron self-will that he exhibited in the face of a steadily growing public outcry against his methods. And the constant bickering, disloyalty and downright disobedience of his *magister equitum* Marcus Minucius Rufus (*cos.* 221 BC), who wanted to throw Fabius' strategy overboard and attack Hannibal, made a difficult situation worse – he himself was to be outfoxed by Hannibal's tactics. Fabius certainly deserved the tribute paid to him by the contemporary poet, Ennius, who described him as 'the one man who restores the state by delaying (*cunctando*)', a line that received the accolade of being immortalized by Virgil (*Aeneid* 6.846 West).

Caius Terentius Varro

The consular elections of 216 BC were held amid scenes of savage bickering and popular demand for strong measures against the Punic invaders (Livy 22.33.9–34.1). It is therefore no surprise that when the first elections were finally held the sole candidate to be elected was Caius Terentius Varro, a strong advocate of meeting Hannibal in battle.

Varro's subsequent defeat has made him the scapegoat of most ancient writers, who have eagerly seized upon suggestions that he was a gutter demagogue, a butcher's son – as Cromwell was called a brewer – and a dangerous fool (Livy 22.25.18–26.4, Plutarch *Fabius Maximus* 14.1, Appian *Hannibalica* 17, Cassius Dio fr. 57.24). These authors have chosen to ignore the Roman senatorial system and have not bothered investigating Varro's previous career too closely. As Lazenby (1978: 74) rightly remarks, it would have been impossible for a butcher's son to be elected to the consulship, and the worst that can be said of Varro in this respect is that he was a *novus homo* rather than from a well-established senatorial family.

He had in fact already served as quaestor (222 BC), aedile (221 BC) and praetor (218 BC), and thus had climbed the established career ladder, the *cursus honorum*, of a Roman aristocrat. Like all those seeking political careers, Varro would have first served in the army at the age of 17. It is also possible that Varro had seen active service in Illyria (219 BC). The picture we are usually given of the vain, arrogant bully who could harangue a meeting but not command an army is therefore somewhat wide of the mark. It would seem that Varro, while certainly no military genius, was no worse a commander than his predecessors, notably the unconventional Caius Flaminius. However, Livy (22.61.14) was quite right to point out that if Varro had

Marble statue of Marcus Claudius Marcellus (Rome, Musei Capitolini), the one opponent of whom Hannibal said: '[he] is the only general who when victorious allows the enemy no rest, and when defeated takes none himself' (Plutarch *Marcellus* 9.4). Having killed Marcellus in an ambush (208 BC), Hannibal recovered the body and had it cremated with due ceremony, the ashes being sent to Marcellus' son in a silver urn (ibid. 30.1-4). He did, however, keep Marcellus' signet ring. (Fields-Carré Collection)

been Carthaginian, he would probably have perished by crucifixion. Yet even after the slaughterhouse that was Cannae, he subsequently commanded an army in Etruria (208 BC, 207 BC).

Lucius Aemilius Paullus (d. 216 BC)

Lucius Aemilius Paullus (*cos.* I 219 BC, *cos.* II 216 BC) was the grandfather of Publius Cornelius Scipio Aemilianus (*cos.* I 147 BC, *cos.* II 134 BC), the destroyer of Carthage (146 BC) and Polybios' chief patron, and as a result receives very favourable treatment from the Greek historian. His detailing of the activities of the Aemilii and Cornelii families is written in order to show them in the best possible light, a key sub-text running through Polybios' narrative of the Hannibalic War. Aemilius Paullus was to fall in battle, but, unlike Caius Flaminius, he was a member of a patrician family, who were more than capable of defending his reputation in later years. This makes it extremely difficult for us to separate propaganda from verity, and so gain some genuine insight into the characters of these men.

Yet by all accounts Aemilius Paullus was a good soldier who had conducted the Illyrian campaign (219 BC) with success and celebrated a triumph (Polybios 3.19.12–13). This campaign, against Demetrios of Pharos, had involved combined operations between the fleet and army as the Romans operated along the Adriatic coast, but there had been no pitched battles (Polybios 3.19.13, Frontinus *Strategemata* 4.1.45). Command in such a low-level conflict certainly made great demands on a general, but the skills required were not precisely the same as those needed to control the field army of 216 BC, which was four times larger than a standard consular army. Even so, as a friend of Quintus Fabius Maximus and an apparent advocate of his delaying tactics, he was elected co-consul to Caius Terentius Varro.

Marcus Claudius Marcellus (271–208 BC)

In 208 BC the stage was set for the first full-scale confrontation with Hannibal since Cannae. But before battle was joined, the consuls were ambushed near Venusia (Venosa) by a band of Numidians; Marcus Claudius Marcellus was killed, and Titus Quinctius Crispinus was mortally wounded (Polybios 10.32.1–6, cf. Livy 27.26.7–11). Marcellus (*cos.* I 222 BC, *cos.* II 214 BC, *cos.* III 210 BC, *cos.* IV 208 BC) had fought with distinction in Sicily during the closing stages of the First Punic War, and was awarded the *corona civica* for saving his brother's life in battle. Arguably the best soldier Rome possessed, it is said that Hannibal feared Fabius as a schoolmaster but regarded Marcellus as an antagonist, for the former prevented him from doing any mischief while the latter might make him suffer it (Plutarch *Marcellus* 9.4). Though obviously not in Hannibal's league as a commander, he was a veteran fighter who was never laid low by defeat and served Rome well, especially in the dark days after Cannae.

Marcellus was certainly far more pugnacious than his contemporary, Fabius, and apart from his military training he was poorly educated – in fact some claimed he was illiterate. During his first consulship he had killed the

Insubrian war chief, Britomarus, in single combat and stripped him of his armour. This heroic deed had won for him the rarest of honours available to a Roman aristocrat, the right to dedicate the third and the last *spolia opima* (spoils of honour) to Iuppiter Feretrius, and his ensuing victory over the Gauls that day earned him a triumph (Plutarch *Marcellus* 6–8 *passim*, *Fasti Triumphales* 531 AUC). During the middle Republic roughly one consul in three celebrated a triumph, but the *spolia opima*, the name given to the spoils taken in personal conflict by a Roman general from the general of the enemy, was much rarer. It was commonly said that Fabius was the shield, while Marcellus was 'the sword of Rome' (Plutarch *Marcellus* 9.4), a fitting tribute for this hero-general.

Publius Cornelius Scipio Africanus (236–185 BC)

Hannibal lost because Rome, with its huge reserves of high-quality manpower, refused to admit defeat even when he had forced it onto its knees. Second, central Italy and its colonies did not revolt and the Gauls, as a nation, did not join him (or his brother Hasdrubal). Third, Carthage failed to gain the command of the sea and dissipated its war effort, to no effect. Fourth, the Cornelii Scipiones confined Hasdrubal Barca to Iberia until 208 BC, and produced the younger Publius Cornelius Scipio (*cos.* I 205 BC, *cos.* II 194 BC), who would later celebrate a triumph and take the cognomen 'Africanus', a soldier whose tactical genius was at least the equal of Hannibal's.

Of course we have to remember the Cornelii Scipiones were one of the most influential of Roman families, and very much a law unto themselves. We only have to think of the way the not-yet-famous Scipio secured the command in Iberia, vacant after the deaths of his father and uncle (211 BC), despite being a private citizen (*privatus*) aged barely 25, and never having held any office higher than that of curule aedile (Polybios 10.4.5, cf. Livy 25.2.6–8). The aedile was a middle-ranking magistrate without military duties, being solely responsible for maintaining roads and aqueducts, supervising traffic and markets and organizing public games and festivals. It was an essential preliminary for those higher offices in Rome, the praetorship and the consulship.

He had seen action aplenty, however, in the sharp cavalry skirmish on the banks of the Ticinus (218 BC), when, according to one tradition, he had single-handedly saved his father's life (Polybios 10.3.3–7, Livy 21.46.7–8). Though there is no record of the part he played in the actual battle, he was also at Cannae (216 BC), where, from Livy's account, it seems he was among those who escaped across the Aufidus to the main Roman camp on the opposite bank. Then, rather than surrender, he was one of the unshaken 4,000 who managed to elude the prowling Carthaginian cavalry patrols and stagger into Canusium. There, in recognition of his leadership during this desperate time – Scipio was serving as military tribune with *legio II* – he was elected by the fugitives to be one of their two commanders (Livy 22.52.4, 53.1, cf. Frontinus *Strategemata* 4.7.39, Valerius Maximus 5.6.7, Silius Italicus *Punica* 10.426–8). Perhaps it was these deeds of derring-do in the face of

Marble head of Publius Cornelius Scipio Africanus (Rome, Musei Capitolini, inv. MC 562). As a general, Scipio blended personal magnetism with careful planning based on good use of intelligence and attention to training, and was not afraid to use innovatory tactics, often based on the element of surprise. Despite his success, however, he would end his life in exile. (Fields-Carré Collection)

Three centuries after Cannae, Juvenal (*Satires* 7.160-4) would write satirically of schoolboys doomed to discuss as rhetorical exercises whether Hannibal ought to have followed his victory by a march on Rome. A view (looking north-west on Piazza dei Cinquecento) of a stretch of the fortifications that defended Rome at the time of Hannibal. The so-called Servian Wall, which actually belongs to the period immediately after the occupation of Rome by the Gaul Brennos (390 BC), ran for some 11km and enclosed an area of roughly 426 hectares. (Fields-Carré Collection)

defeatist machinations that inspired the Roman people to invest him *imperium pro consule* to conduct the war in Iberia (Livy 26.18.9).

Scipio was an inspiring leader who could gain and keep the loyalty of his men. His charismatic character and judicious diplomacy won him many allies, without whom Rome might not have won the war. Seeing the deficiencies of the rather static traditional Roman tactics, Scipio experimented with small tactical units that could operate with greater flexibility. His tactics were inspired by Hannibal's and needed good legionary officers as well as generalship to implement. He thus saw the value of capable subordinates who could proceed on their own initiative. His realistic tactical appraisal remade the Roman Army under his command into a force that made better use of its inherent strengths.

Scipio's strategy of striking at Punic forces in Iberia, and letting the conquest of ground take care of itself, was brilliant, and was in complete contrast to that of his predecessors. But although he has been extravagantly praised for his strategy in invading Africa, this had been the Roman plan since 218 BC, and appears pedestrian in comparison with Hannibal's daring invasion of Italy and rapid succession of victories. To utter an impertinent truth, the strategy Scipio pursued in Africa was by no means original, for he was merely following in the footsteps of Agathokles and Regulus. It is easy for us to be critical, however, and Scipio's methods paid off in the end, particularly in drawing Hannibal inland away from his secure base by the sea, and also in the ravaging of the fertile and populous Bagradas Valley with fire and sword, which probably forced Hannibal into battle before he was ready.

Scipio was to adopt the cognomen 'Africanus' by virtue of his achievement at Zama, apparently the first Roman general to be known by a name derived from the scene of his victories. Though Livy, our authority here, says he was unable 'to find out how it became current – through the army's devotion to their general, or from popular favour; or it may have started with the flattery of his close friends, in the way, in our fathers' time, Sulla was called "Felix" and Pompey "Magnus". What is certain is that Scipio was the first general to be celebrated by the name of the people he conquered' (30.45.6–7). Seneca, however, states (*de brevitate vitae* 13.5) that the consul Marcus Valerius Maximus, who captured Messana (263 BC), adopted the name 'Messana', which was afterwards changed to 'Messala'.

Both men were fine tacticians but Ilipa (206 BC), Scipio's most tactically sophisticated battle, appears cumbersome when compared with Cannae. Hannibal himself is supposed to have said to Scipio that, if he had won Zama, he would have rated himself even better than Alexander, Pyrrhos and all the rest, thereby deliberately flattering them both (Livy 35.14.9, cf. Plutarch *Flamininus* 21.3–4). That is debatable, but few would agree with Suvorov (no doubt echoing Polybios, who is perhaps more generous than wise here) that Scipio was the better general, even though he won the battle, which in truth was little more than a traditional slogging match. It is always difficult to assess correctly the stature of a commander who was beaten in the end, and historians tend to assume that he is inevitably inferior to the commander who beat him, forgetting the circumstances that may have brought about that defeat. Much like Robert E. Lee, whom most people agree was a splendid man, Hannibal was beaten, not by a better general, but by a better army. Great soldier as Scipio was, in almost every respect he falls short of the rank attained by Hannibal. In truth, there was no one in that period who could match the Carthaginian's experience in war, the breadth of his strategic vision or his tactical capabilities in all the configurations of land warfare.

INSIDE THE MIND

After the crushingly one-sided success at Cannae, says Livy, Maharbal boasted to his victorious commander-in-chief that he, at the head of the cavalry, could ride to Rome where Hannibal should be 'dining, in triumph, on the Capitol within five days'. Hannibal, although he commends his cavalry commander's zeal, demurs. Maharbal retorts by saying that Hannibal knew how to win a fight, but did not know how use the victory. 'This day's delay,' Livy piously concludes, 'is generally believed to have been the salvation of the city and the empire' (22.51.5,6).

With the hindsight we enjoy – which was already available to Livy – it would be easy for us to agree with him and find fault with Hannibal for not at once marching on Rome after Cannae and capturing the city by a *coup de main*. Hoyos, intriguingly perhaps, floats the suggestion that the Maharbal story does not belong to the aftermath of Cannae, it having been displaced from Trasimene, 'a battlefield 85 miles [137km], four days' march, from Rome, not 300 miles [483km] like Cannae' (2008: 53, cf. 60). However, let us not judge him – as we are all too prone to judge – on insufficient knowledge, and see what his chances were. Rome was some 480km away, a distance that would take over three weeks to cover with the army marching at a forced rate of 20km a day, ample time for the Romans to organize the defence of the well-walled city. Moreover, Rome

Marble statue of Hannibal at Schloss Schönbrunn, Vienna. Hannibal did not like to start a battle unless he had it all planned out in his head and knew he was going to win. In a very real sense Hannibal stands out from the common crowd – the 'sand of humanity' as Nietzsche so caustically put it – by his deeds and by his example. (Author's collection)

Hannibal betrachtet den Kopf des Hasdrubal (Vienna, Kunsthistorisches Museum), decorative panel (1725–30) by Giambattista Tiepolo (1696–1770). Hasdrubal had left Iberia for Italy, but was run to ground near the Metaurus, where he and his command went down fighting (207 BC). The first news that Hannibal received of the fate of his reinforcements was his brother's head, carefully preserved, thrown into his camp by the Romans. (The Yorck Project)

still had two legions sitting within the city itself, and a fleet stationed at Ostia, which raised a legion of marines after the appalling catastrophe of Cannae, while 8,000 able-bodied slaves were purchased and armed by the state (Livy 22.57.7–8). It must also be remembered that the Roman Army was a citizen force; the population of Rome could be armed from any available source and by this means defend the walls of their city.

In truth, throughout antiquity very few cities fell to a direct assault and, in the main, they were captured either through treachery or by conducting a long and drawn-out siege, the eight-month siege of Saguntum being typical. The hazard of direct assault actually involved the besieger finding a way over, through or under the fortifications of the besieged, and so what the besieger often did was to shut the besieged off, and let disease, hunger or thirst, usually all three, do his work for him. As Philip II of Macedon once said, the best way to take a city is with asses heavily laden with gold (cf. Demosthenes *On the Crown* 246–7). Moreover, Hannibal may well have recalled what had happened to Pyrrhus some 60 years earlier when, having won a victory on the broad plains near Herakleia, he advanced to within 60km of Rome only to withdraw empty-handed. Having said all that, if Hannibal marched away from southern Italy he would have left an area that was offering him vital support in his war with Rome. No part of Hannibal's long-term strategy involved a march on Rome, and even in 211 BC, when he came right up to its gates, he was tempting the Romans to lift their siege of Capua (cf. Livy 26.7–11 *passim*, Frontinus *Strategemata* 3.18.2–3, Valerius Maximus 3.7.10).

There is the criticism amongst modern observers and military pundits that Hannibal was unable to capture the cities of southern Italy. This is valid only to a point. Hannibal was clearly attempting to win allies to his cause, and the indiscriminate sacking of cities – which was the fate of two, Nuceria and Acerrae (Livy 23.15.1–6, Cassius Dio 15.37.30, 34, Zonaras 9.2) – would hardly have endeared him to the Italic peoples. It has also been said that Hannibal failed to capture cities because he lacked a siege train. A siege train was not a requirement for a successful general in ancient warfare, as he had only to construct his siege machinery *in situ* (cf. Livy 29.6, the siege of Locri). Besides, Hannibal's idea of warfare was one of mobility, and he certainly did not envisage himself being strategically hampered through having to conduct lengthy sieges.

Yet another criticism levelled against Hannibal was his lack of understanding of the importance of sea-power. This can be easily dismissed because he had certainly intended to rendezvous with the Carthaginian fleet at Pisae (Pisa) during the summer of 217 BC (Polybios

3.96.9), but had missed the opportunity to do so as he was otherwise busy at Lake Trasimene, where he was demolishing the consular army of Caius Flaminius. Hannibal also captured a number of seaports in southern Italy, the greatest being that of Tarentum, but the Carthaginian navy failed in supporting him throughout the war; it was far away, slow to take action and tardy in bringing help. The one notable exception to this was its successful landing of 4,000 Numidian reinforcements (including 40 elephants) at Locri in 215 BC (Livy 23.13.7, 41.10, 43.6).

On the other hand, the war itself revealed the latent power of Rome – that is, its hydra-like capacity to produce men. Most of Rome's previous wars had been fought with two consular armies each of two legions and their usual complement of Latin-Italian *alae* and, as Polybios emphasizes (3.107.9, cf. Livy 22.36.2–4), when eight legions were mobilized for the Cannae campaign this had never before been done. But if Polybios is right in stating there were eight legions at Cannae, Rome had already mobilized a total of ten legions, since there were already two in Iberia, and by 211 BC there were to be 25 legions under arms in the different theatres of war, 16 in Italy itself, which, taking the *alae* and the men serving at sea into consideration, represented something like 250,000 men (Brunt 1971: 419–22). As Kineas,

View from the ribat over the medina quarter looking south-east towards the kasbah (AD 589) in Sousse, Tunisia. Known as Hadrumetum to the Romans, the city was to serve as Hannibal's base during the final phases of his long, exhausting war with Rome.
(Ancient Art & Architecture)

Reverse of a Punic silver coin (London, British Museum), from the Mogente Hoard, Valencia, dated *c.*230 BC. Minted in southern Iberia by the Barca family, it depicts the elephant regularly employed by the Carthaginians, the small African forest elephant (*Loxodonta africana cyclotis*). Hannibal and his elephants became to the Romans legendary symbols of an overwhelming alien power. (Fields-Carré Collection).

the trusted diplomat of Pyrrhos, was said to have predicted, the many-headed monster could regenerate and struggle on (Plutarch *Pyrrhos* 19.7).

At the killing fields of Cannae Rome lost, according to Livy (for once his figures are less sweeping than those of Polybios), nearly 50,000 troops; or, to put it more bluntly, its army had suffered some 80 per cent casualties. The casualty rate suffered by Britain and its colonial allies on 1 July 1916, the date of the opening of the British offensive on the river Somme, does not compare with this shocking figure (19,240 killed, 35,493 wounded, 2,152 posted as missing and 585 captured). No other state in antiquity could have survived such a shattering defeat. At the time of the Gallic troubles, which flared up some seven years before Hannibal's arrival, Rome, according to Polybios, could mobilize 700,000 infantry and 70,000 cavalry, whereas Hannibal invaded Italy with only 20,000 infantry and 6,000 cavalry (Polybios 2.24.16–17, cf. 3.33.17–18, 56.4). This inexhaustible supply of manpower is one primary reason why Rome ultimately defeated Hannibal, while another is the steadfastness of the Roman people. They were placed into dire situations that would have produced, at the very least, treachery in any other ancient state. Look at, for example, Rome's blunt refusal to ransom its prisoners after the humiliation of Cannae (Livy 22.58, cf. 26.11). As the poet Ennius, who had reached manhood about this time, would write soon after in a memorable line: 'The victor is not victorious if the vanquished does not consider himself so' (*Annales* fr. 493 Vahlen).

It is almost certain that Hannibal did not envisage a final triumph amongst the smoking ruins of a sacked and gutted Rome. His strategy was not a merciless one, a matter of letting nothing survive. At the Trebbia and at Lake Trasimene, Polybios (3.77.3–7, 85.1–4, cf. Frontinus *Strategemata* 4.7.25) clearly shows him courteously releasing his Latin-Italian prisoners of war without ransom money having been demanded of them, sending them home with the message that he had come to emancipate Italy from the yoke of Rome and to hand back the territories it had stolen. Livy also has Hannibal continuing this policy after Cannae, adding that Hannibal addressed his Roman prisoners and stressed that he was not fighting to destroy them, but 'for honour and hegemony' (22.58.1–2, 3). Though he may have sworn eternal hatred of them, Hannibal was not planning to exterminate the Romans.

Two facts support this hypothesis. First, Hannibal, after Cannae, attempted to open negotiations with Rome. Indeed, he had expected the Romans to send the overtures for peace, it being the obvious thing to do because if they fought on he would defeat them again, and meanwhile more and more of their allies would be deserting them. In three years he had mauled successive armies sent against him and marched wherever he wished in Italy. Second,

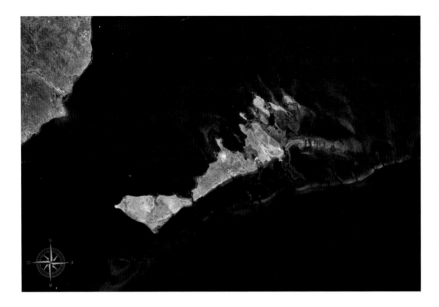

an article in the sworn treaty between Philip V of Macedon and Carthage shows Rome being stripped of its allies but allowed to exist as a Latin state of little consequence and held in check by those who had just had their autonomy restored to them (Polybios 7.9.12–15). Hannibal's aim was to disrupt Rome's confederacy and thereby drag it battered and shrunken to the negotiating table, where it would then be stripped of any remaining allies and burdened with a crippling war indemnity. With Rome reduced to the status of a second-rate power, rather than that of a major player in the Mediterranean, Carthage would have been able to regain Sicily, Sardinia and its other lost territories, as well as having a free hand in mineral-rich Iberia. Everything that Hannibal did was subject to this principle, and undertaken with this objective, using military means only as an instrument, albeit a very powerful one, to achieve it.

WHEN WAR IS DONE

Livy, in a famous passage (21.4), almost likens the not-yet-famous Hannibal to Antaeus, invigorated by contact with the earth, describing him as one of the healthiest, most vital men who ever lived, almost immune to hunger and thirst, heat and cold, sleepiness and fatigue. He adds that 'he was often to be seen, wrapped in an army cloak, asleep on the ground amid common soldiers on sentry or picket duties' (21.4.9). Of course, Livy depicts an idealized portrait of the young general, which may be seen as a kind of heroic stereotype. A legend in his own time, the young general rapidly assumed bizarre proportions in Roman folklore, an imaginative mythology generously coloured with death, deceit and diabolism. What we are dealing with, in short, is a stock motif.

In truth the great general has to be studied not only as a strategist but also as a tactician, an organizer, a leader of men and sometimes even as a statesman. Returned to civilian life, Hannibal now had the opportunity to employ his great powers of statesmanship, no longer masked by his prestigious soldierly skills. There was plenty of scope for it in his politically bankrupt and physically exhausted country. One of his first tasks, after his appointment as one of the two *sufetes*, was to have an investigation made of the resources left to Carthage. The situation in fact was far better than could be expected. The city was on the road to recovery with regards to its commercial prosperity, but before long a scandal broke out. The first instalment of the war indemnity due to Rome under the terms of the peace treaty was paid in 199 BC, but the silver was found to be of such poor quality that Carthage had to make up the deficiency by borrowing money in Rome (Livy 32.2.1). In looking into the scandal, Hannibal soon found himself up against the ruling council. He obtained a major revision of the constitution, and the council was subject to annual elections with the proviso that no man should hold office for two consecutive years.

By eradicating administrative corruption and functionary embezzlement, and collecting arrears of unpaid taxes, Hannibal showed how the heavy war indemnity could be paid without increasing public taxation (Livy 33.46.1–47.2). Government putrescence and peculation was scarcely novel in Carthage, but Hannibal's far-reaching reforms, which also embraced commerce and agriculture, were so successful that by 191 BC Carthage could offer to pay off the whole of the outstanding debt – 40 years' instalments – in a lump sum (namely 8,000 talents), while also supplying the Roman army currently at war in the eastern Mediterranean with large quantities of grain. The offer, either for reasons of spite or arrogance, was disdainfully declined (Livy 36.4.7). Interestingly, according to Aurelius Victor, a 4th-century writer from Roman Africa, Hannibal had even turned his soldiers to agriculture. He writes that Hannibal 'replanted much of Africa with olive trees, using his soldiers, whose idleness he considered problematic for Carthage and its leaders' (*Liber de Caesaribus* 37.3).

Hannibal had another and more tricky situation to deal with. When his brother's army left Liguria, a Carthaginian officer with the name of Hamilcar stayed behind and placed himself at the head of a number of malcontent Ligurian and Gaulish tribes. The Latin colonies of Plancentia and Cremona were attacked. Rome naturally complained to Carthage, demanding the recall and surrender of this freebooter, whose activities were a clear breach of the peace treaty. Suspicion, naturally, was laid on Hannibal of having taken some dastardly part in these guerilla operations in Gallia Cisalpina, but the senate in Carthage replied that it had no power to do anything beyond exiling this Hamilcar and confiscating his property.

Meanwhile, in the aftermath of Hannibal's defeat, the Romans had turned their attention towards the east. Ostensibly in response to appeals from the tiny, but independent, powers of Pergamon and Rhodes, Rome decided to intervene in Greece before Philip V of Macedon (r. 221–179 BC) and

There is another tradition that the footloose military genius went to the newly independent kingdom of Armenia before going on to Crete. Here, according to both Strabo (11.14.6) and Plutarch (*Lucullus* 31.4–5), the satrap-turned-king, Artaxias, having no military tasks for Hannibal, had him survey a site for his new capital by the river Araxes beneath Mount Ararat, the soon-to-be Artaxata (Artashat). This is a view of Khorvirap Monastery, Armenia, with the twin peaks of Büyük Ara Dağı (5,165m) and Küçük Ara Dağı (3,925m) of Mount Ararat in the distance. (Author's collection)

Antiochos III of Syria (r. 223–187 BC) had a chance to upset the balance of power in the east. This is an example of Rome's increasing propensity to regard other people's business as its own, viewing events in regions bordering on its sphere of influence as events upon which its was entitled, at the very least, to voice an opinion. The possession of irresistible power tends to lead to such arrogance. Rome had never forgiven Philip for his alliance with Hannibal, naturally, but Antiochos was very different.

One of the greatest Hellenistic monarchs who – in conscious imitation of Alexander – bore the epithet 'the Great', Antiochos earned this title attempting to reconstitute the kingdom by bringing back into the fold the former outlying possessions. He thus managed to reassert the power of the Seleukid dynasty briefly in the upper satrapies and Anatolia, which effectively made him ruler of the eastern world from the Indus to the Aegean, but then inadvisably challenged Rome for control of Greece in 194 BC. Concerned first and foremost with maintaining in their entirety the territorial possessions he had inherited from his forefathers, having just retrieved them, what Antiochos wanted was for Rome to mind its own business and leave him free to do as he wished on his side of the Hellespont. It was not to be. Towards the end of 190 BC Rome, backed by Pergamon and Rhodes, won the final battle over Antiochos on the level plain of Magnesia in Lydia, driving that magnificent and ambitious king back across the Taurus mountains and out of Anatolia. According to Livy (37.1.7–10, cf. Cicero *Philippics* 11.17), a public announcement by Scipio Africanus that he was going to serve as his brother's legate secured the Asian command for Lucius Cornelius Scipio (*cos.* 190 BC), particularly as it was widely known in Rome that Hannibal was in Antiochos' court. This highly organized man, of rare precocity, comes over as an all-time manipulator of public opinion.

In fact the old adversaries did not encounter each other again in battle, nor was Scipio Africanus present at Magnesia (Scullard 1970: 210–44).

It was suspected in Rome that Hannibal had been in touch with Antiochos. This would of course have been another breach of the peace treaty by which Carthage was bound not to partake in any hostilities without Rome's acquiescence, especially not when they appeared to be directed against Rome itself. Rome had another reason to be furious with Hannibal, for his skill in reorganizing the finances of Carthage had made the Roman plans miscarry; they had hoped that the war indemnity would cripple Carthage, and they were disappointed. Despite the reasonable objections of Scipio Africanus, a commission was sent to Carthage in 195 BC (the very year Marcus Porcius Cato, the elder Cato as he is known to history, was consul) alleging that Hannibal was aiding an enemy of Rome. In the senatorial debate Scipio Africanus brought his full weight to bear against those he saw lending a favourable ear to what he viewed as a baseless accusation, 'considering that it consorted ill with the dignity of the Roman people to associate themselves with the animosities of Hannibal's accusers, [and] to add the support of official backing to the factions at Carthage' (Livy 33.47.4). Noble words, but they fell on deaf ears.

Be that as it may, at this very moment Hannibal's position in Carthage was insecure. For not only had he made implacable enemies of all those functionaries whose peculations and perks he had stopped, but his year of office as *sufete* had now expired. And so, with his keen sense of appreciation that the Roman commissioners could not fail to demand his surrender, along with the probability that the Carthaginian senate would comply, he withdrew from their grasp by a series of characteristic tricks. Pretending to be going for a short ride with two trusted companions (possibly Sosylos and Silenos), he rode through the night, hell for leather, to his seaside estate near Thapsus – more than 150km as the crow flies. His treasure had already been embarked on a fully outfitted and crewed ship, and he sailed for Cercina, an archipelago just off the coast. There he was recognized by the crews of some Phoenician merchantmen, which was unwelcome to him as the news of his presence there could not fail to reach Carthage. In order to forestall them, Hannibal suggested to the Phoenician ships' captains that they should dine with him on shore and bring their sails and yards with them to provide shelter from the midsummer sun, which they did. What they did not realize was that by doing so they had delayed the time of their departure the next day.

Naturally, Hannibal showed a clean pair of heels during the night while the revellers slept off their drink. Back in Carthage the Roman commissioners were furious, and Hannibal's enemies in the Carthaginian senate placated them by formally declaring him to be an outlaw, confiscating his possessions (such as he had left behind him), and razing his property to the ground (Nepos *Hannibal* 7.6–7, Livy 33.45.6–7, 47.3–49.8). There is a Turkish proverb that goes: 'A man who tells the truth is expelled from the seven villages.' So was Hannibal honoured in his own country.

Hannibal sailed away to Antiochos, who must have been an attractive host to him because he was soon to be engaged in fighting the Romans. By accusing him of plotting war with Antiochos, his enemies in Carthage and in Rome (the senators), determined on his downfall, had propelled him into the king's arms. Hannibal caught up with the busy monarch in Ephesos, and there, it is said, explained to him his grandiose plan for opposing Rome. If we are to believe Livy (34.60.3–6, cf. Appian *Syrica* 7, Justin *Epitome* 31.3.7–10), it involved entrusting to Hannibal an army of 10,000 infantry and 1,000 cavalry and a fleet of 100 warships, with which he would first sail to Africa to win over Carthage, and then on to Italy to raise war there against the Romans. At the same time Antiochos was to lead his main army into Greece, where he would take up a strong position to hamper Rome's efforts.

It seems the Romans got wind of Hannibal's war plan, and a combination of artful agents and covetous courtiers scuppered his chances to carry the upcoming war into Rome's backyard (Frontinus *Strategemata* 1.8.7, cf. Livy 35.14.1–2, Nepos *Hannibal* 2.2). As we have noted, Antiochos was eventually defeated at Magnesia, and Rome predictably demanded the surrender of their most implacable foe. When Hannibal had resumed the struggle against the Romans, the outlaw, in their eyes, had become a renegade. Semantics aside, it was too late anyway, for the crafty Hannibal had already embarked his treasure onto a ship and sailed away again, this time for Crete.

Hannibal lived quite comfortably there, but being one not fain to take life calmly as it comes, he was not likely to want to live there for too long. We next find him offering his services to Prusias I of Bithynia (r. 228–181 BC),

This lone Doric column marks the site of the temple of Hera Lacinia on the Lacinian promontory (Capo Colonne). It was here that Hannibal placed an inscription in Punic and Greek recounting the deeds of him and his army in Italy. It also recorded the strength of his army when it first set foot in the peninsula. A generation later it was seen and read by Polybios. (Fototeca ENIT) who was at war with his neighbour Eumenes II of Pergamon (r. 197–158 BC), an ally of Rome who had fought at the battle of Magnesia. This local spat gave Hannibal one last opportunity to show his military genius. Prusias was defeated on land and transferred hostilities to the sea. Outnumbered in ships, Hannibal advised the king's marines to gather venomous snakes, stuff them in earthenware pots, and catapult them onto the enemy's ships. The sailors of Pergamon began by jeering at such ridiculous tactics of fighting with pots instead of swords. But when these pots crashed on board the Pergamene ships, which were soon crawling with snakes, the laugh was on the other side of their faces and, as Justin relates, 'they yielded the victory' (*Epitome* 32.4, cf. Nepos *Hannibal* 10–11 *passim*).

There followed yet another demand for Hannibal's surrender, whom the Romans pursued, as Plutarch says, 'like a bird that had grown too old to fly and had lost its tail feathers' (*Flamininus* 21.1). He was then 64 years old. Hannibal headed off his captors by taking poison, and in his final agony, or so said Livy, he cried out: 'Let us free the Roman people from their long-standing anxiety, seeing that they find it tedious to wait for an old man's death' (39.51.9, cf. Plutarch *Flamininus* 20.5, Nepos *Hannibal* 12). True or not, whether this exit line occurred to him spontaneously or whether he had rehearsed it is not known. Since nobody truly knows what happened, Livy's vision of Hannibal's end is as good as any.

So perished Hannibal of unhappy memory. The year was 183 BC, and there is little doubt that a certain higher authority in Rome breathed freely for the first time since that day, some 35 years back, when Hannibal crossed the Alps. There was no room for forgiveness in the hearts of the Roman nation; they had been too frightened for that. There are some things that can never be forgiven, let alone forgotten.

A LIFE IN WORDS

There is that anecdote that when Hannibal was almost at Rome's gates, the campfires of his alien army clearly visible from the Capitol, a piece of land upon which he was encamped happened to be for sale. It was sold at the usual market price (Livy 26.11.7–8, Frontinus *Strategemata* 3.18.2). 'It was not before the Carthaginian soldiers that Rome was made to tremble, but before Hannibal', so wrote his spiritual brother in arms, Napoleon (*Mémoires*, vol. II, p. 90). Still, some of the anecdotes and biographies that deal with the great captains of history should be viewed as romantic embellishments, anachronistic, or simply dubious. Having said that, we historians still indulge ourselves with erudite tales of the great and near-great in much of what we write, and in doing so still have the habit of improving our images by judicious chiselling and burnishing. In rearranging the past what becomes important for us is the overall rhythm of the life of a would-be great captain, and the mythical aura of an exemplum rather than factual accuracy.

From legends do men draw ideas necessary to their existence, Anatole France once remarked. Yet with Hannibal, as with any other signal historical figures, we should not depict the lives of millions being determined by the masterful will of a single actor. As the Greeks say, or used to say: like the chorus, one man may lead, but many play. Naturally, to do this with Hannibal, we have to sift the reality of his life from the fable and fantasy, so removing him from the malleable domain of legend to the more resistant context of factual record. The reality is more potent than the myth.

Take the Romans for instance, who tended to cast shadows on the Carthaginians by stressing their cruelty and perfidy and the like, and saw Hannibal as a fire-breathing, blood-seeking warmonger indulging in a slavering appetite for violence and revenge. The lettered Seneca did not hesitate to relay one of those snippets that show the Carthaginian in the most odious light: on the eve of battle, seeing a blood-filled ditch, Hannibal exclaimed 'Oh, what a lovely sight' (de ira 2.5.4). The Romans could never forgive Hannibal for having put himself, like a single-minded adventurer, at the head of a fantastic barbarian rabble, leading it from one victory to another. His very name had a menacing ring for them. It fell across the blood-soaked history of Rome like a dark shadow. Thus did Hannibal, Rome's predestined enemy, metamorphose into the ogre of fairy tale, a bogeyman for little Roman children and the stuff of nightmares. In the collective consciousness of nations exceptional figures are invariably despised.

'Wounded Gaul' (Paris, musée du Louvre, inv. MR 133), Roman copy of an earlier Greek bronze.
In the *omnium gatherum* that was his army, it would appear that Hannibal used his Celtic allies (mainly Gauls from northern Italy) as 'cannon fodder', suffering the casualties and receiving few rewards. Yet this wild, warlike race fought in an undisciplined throng, rushing and swinging long swords, and it would be altogether wrong to think that Hannibal rode to victory over the backs of his fallen 'barbarian' friends. (Fields-Carré Collection)

When, in 211 BC, Hannibal stood outside the gates of Rome, such a terrifying moment was not to occur again until the Visigoth Alaric penetrated and pillaged the 'eternal city' in AD 410, a time, some would argue, when Rome's martial fury had long waned and a love of ease and luxury had well and truly taken over. It comes as no surprise, therefore, to learn that among its enemies Rome's chief *bête noire* was beyond question Hannibal, and the proverb *Hannibal ad portas* ('Hannibal is at the gates') would retain its efficacy as a rallying cry for Romans in times of national crisis (e.g. Cicero *de finibus* 4.9.22, *Philippics* 1.5.11, Juvenal *Satires* 6.290, cf. 10.156), and would do so again and again until the very end of the empire. It almost seems as though the Romans did not want their enemy absolutely eliminated.

There is one notable exception to all this white-hot hostility, and that is our Greek friend, Polybios. Writing about five decades after the war with Hannibal, his point of view, and his determination to adopt a position as objective as possible towards the Carthaginians, is best exemplified by the picture he has given us of the man who was in a sense their symbol, Hannibal (9.22.8–10, 24–26 *passim*). Take this Polybian anecdote, for example. In one council of war the question of logistics during the approaching march to Italy via the Alps was raised once again, and one of Hannibal's senior officers, Hannibal's unrelated namesake, nicknamed Monomachos, suggested that the problem could be eased by training the men to survive off human flesh. Hannibal appreciated the practical value of cannibalism but could not bring himself to consider it. There is little doubt that there was much injustice and brutality, for that is how soldiers behave in a conquered land, but Polybios recognized that the reputation for ferocious cruelty, which the Romans attached to Hannibal, may in reality have been due to his having been mistaken for Hannibal Monomachos (9.24.5–8). Here we can pinpoint the trait of *inhumana crudelitas*, enthusiastically sketched by Livy as one of the chief components in his moral portrait of Hannibal (21.4). Of course, as a good Roman, Livy had no liking for Hannibal.

Though the public are fascinated by a battle in which one army is exterminated, the account thereof can read much like a classic morality play. Close students of warfare regard Cannae as a classic example of a successful double-envelopment manoeuvre. This Hannibalic masterpiece, the most perfect tactical battle ever fought, is a lesson in annihilation striven after by many military commanders (at best eager pupils) and, for that reason, continues to be assiduously studied in military academy classrooms. Wellington attempted the technique at Vitoria (1813), and Napoleon had almost achieved it at Ulm (1805), writing: 'Not one is to escape' (*Correspondance*, vol. XI, no. 9374, p. 318). The problem was that no modern European army, not even the Grande Armée, could move fast enough or coordinate the movements of the different columns sufficiently to close the trap before the enemy took evasive action. Also, Hannibal had created the illusion that the impossible was possible for men who were merely highly talented.

Clausewitz wrote that 'Concentric operations are simply unsuited to the weaker side' (*Vom Krieg* 6.25), and Napoleon (despite Ulm) felt that Hannibal's murderous trap was too risky and that it was the product more of luck than genius. Luck may be just luck, as everybody knows, yet more often it is the result of ability, instinct or knowledge. On the other hand, for others Cannae became an *idée fixe*. The Prussian strategist Graf Alfred von Schlieffen was obsessed with Hannibal's victory, finding it reassuring that the intellect of one man could nullify the discipline, proficiency and sheer numerical superiority of thousands. As the architect of the plan used for the German invasion of France in August 1914, he analysed the battle time and time again for inspiration as he painstakingly drafted and redrafted his grand design.

The 'Schlieffen Plan' (in truth, a series of yearly memoranda) envisaged a Cannae on a gigantic scale, a wheel through Belgium with a neutral frontier and mountain ranges replacing the second envelopment wing. The resultant plan bore only a superficial similarity to Hannibal's tactics at Cannae and was conceived on an infinitely grander scale. It was to be a strategical envelopment: a right hook through Belgium to deliver a rapid decision in France (i.e. in about 40 days) before major operations were undertaken against the Russian Army, which would be much slower to mobilize. The plan failed. To be fair, however, in the very same month but in another theatre of operations, the remarkable duet of Hindenburg and Ludendorff did succeed in reproducing the Cannae principle of envelopment when they met the Russian Second Army in the battle of Tannenberg. The Russian centre was allowed to advance, then the Germans drove in both flanks, encircled the Second Army and practically wiped it out. Of course, no single commander will ever be able to replicate Hannibal's impact on battlefield tactics. The battle of Cannae, a chef-d'oeuvre of battlefield tactics, is the consummate Hannibalic canvas, one that has no superior, and perhaps no equal either.

BIBLIOGRAPHY

Ardent du Picq, C., (translated by Greely, Colonel J. and Cotton, Major R., 1920), *Battle Studies: Ancient and Modern,* US Army War College: Harrisburg, 1903; repr. 1946

Astin, A. E., 'Saguntum and the origins of the Second Punic War' in *Latomus* 26: 577–96, 1967

Bagnall, N., *The Punic Wars: Rome, Carthage and the Struggle for the Mediterranean,* Pimlico: London, 1990; repr. 1999

Bath, T., *Hannibal's Campaigns,* Cambridge: Patrick Stephens, 1981

Beer, G. de, *Hannibal's March,* Sidgwick & Jackson: London, 1967

——, *Hannibal,* Thames & Hudson: London, 1969

Brunt, P. A., *Italian Manpower, 225 BC – AD 14,* Oxford University Press: Oxford, 1971

Carey, B. T., Allfree, J. B. and Cairns, J., *Warfare in the Ancient World,* Pen & Sword: Barnsley, 2005

Connolly, P., *Greece and Rome at War,* Stackpole: Mechanicsburg, PA, 1981; repr. 1998

Cornell, T. J., Rankov, N. B. and Sabin, P. (eds.), *The Second Punic War: A Reappraisal*, Bulletin of the Institute of Classical Studies 67, University of London Press: London, 1996

Daly, G., *Cannae: The Experience of Battle in the Second Punic War*, Routledge: London, 2002

Dawson, D., *The Origins of Western Warfare*, Westview: Boulder, CO, 1996

Dodge, T. A., *The Great Captains*, Strong Oak Press: Stevenage, 1889; repr. 2002

Febvre, L., *La terre et l'évolution humaine*, Paris, 1922; repr. 1970

Fields, N., *The Roman Army of the Punic Wars, 264 – 146 BC*, Osprey: Oxford, 2007

——, *Carthaginian Warrior, 264–146 BC*, Osprey: Oxford, 2010

——, *Roman Conquests: North Africa*, Pen & Sword: Barnsley, 2010

Fuller, J. F. C., *The Generalship of Alexander the Great*, De Capo Press: New York, 1960; repr. 1989

Gaebel, R. E., *Cavalry Operations in the Ancient Greek World*, University of Oklahoma Press: Norman, OK, 2002

Garouphalias, P., *Pyrrhus, King of Epirus*, Stacy International: London, 1979

Goldsworthy, A. K., *The Punic Wars*, Cassell: London, 2000

——, *Cannae*, Cassell: London, 2001

——, *In the Name of Rome: The Men Who Won the Roman Empire*, Phoenix: London, 2003; repr. 2004

Grainger, J. D., *The Roman War of Antiochus the Great*, Brill: Leiden/Boston, 2002

Griffith, G. T., *The Mercenaries of the Hellenistic World*, Ares Publishers: Chicago, 1935; repr. 1984

Gsell, S., *Histoire ancienne de l' Afrique du Nord*, vol. 2, Paris, 1928

Head, D., *Armies of the Macedonian and Punic Wars, 359 BC – 146 BC*, Wargames Research Group: Worthing, 1982

Hoyos, D., *Hannibal's Dynasty: Power and Politics in the Western Mediterranean, 247–183 BC*, Routledge: London, 2003; repr. 2005

——, *Hannibal: Rome's Greatest Enemy*, Bristol Phoenix Press: Exeter, 2008

Jones, B. W., 'Rome's relationship with Carthage: a study in aggression' in *The Classical Bulletin* 49: 5–26, Bolchazy-Carducci Publishers: Mundelein, IL, 1972

Kistler, J. M., *War Elephants*, Praeger Publishers: Westport, CT, 2005

Lancel, S., (translated by Nevill, A., 1995), *Carthage*, Blackwell: Oxford, 1992

——, (translated by Nevill, A., 1998), *Hannibal*, Blackwell: Oxford, 1995; repr. 1999

Lazenby, J. F., *Hannibal's War: A Military History of the Second Punic War*, Aris & Phillips: Warminster, 1978

——, *The First Punic War: A Military History*, University College London Press: London, 1996

Liddell Hart, B. H., *Scipio Africanus: Greater than Napoleon*, De Capo Press: New York, 1926; repr. 1994

Moscati, S. (ed.), *The Phoenicians*, I. B. Tauris: London, 1997; repr. 2001

Nossov, K. S., *War Elephants*, Osprey: Oxford, 2008

Picard, C. G. and Picard, C., (translated by Collon, D., 1969), *The Life and Death of Carthage*, Sidgwick and Jackson Ltd: London, 1968

Proctor, D., *Hannibal's March in History*, Oxford University Press: Oxford, 1971

Ridley, R. J., 'Was Scipio Africanus at Cannae?' in *Latomus* 34: 161–5, 1975

Sanctis, G. de, *Storia dei Romani*, vol. 3.2, Kessinger Publishing: Florence, 1968

Scullard, H. H., *Scipio Africanus, Soldier and Politician*, Thames & Hudson: London, 1970

——, *The Elephant in the Greek and Roman World*, Thames & Hudson: London, 1974

Seibert, J., *Hannibal*, Wissenschaftliche Buchgesellschaft: Darmstadt, 1993

Sumner, G. V., 'Roman policy in Spain before the Hannibalic War' in *Harvard Studies in Classical Philology*, vol. 72, pp. 205–46, Harvard, 1967

Walbank, F. W., *A Historical Commentary on Polybios*, vol. 1, Clarendon Press: Oxford, 1957

——, *A Historical Commentary on Polybios*, vol. 2, Clarendon Press: Oxford, 1970

Warry, J., *Warfare in the Classical World*, Salamander: London, 1980

Wise, T. and Healy, M., *Hannibal's War with Rome: The Armies and Campaigns 216 BC*, Osprey: Oxford, 1999; repr. 2001

GLOSSARY

ager publicus	'public land' – state-owned land acquired by conquest
AUC	*ab urbe condita*, meaning 'from the founding of the city [Rome]', reckoned from 21 April 753 BC
ala/alae	'wing' – Latin/Italian unit comparable to *legio* (q.v.)
hastati	'spearmen' – young legionaries forming the front line of a manipular legion of the middle Republic
legio/legiones	'levy' – principal unit of the Roman Army
magister equitum	'master of horse' – second in command to dictator
maniple	tactical unit of a manipular legion of the middle Republic
novus homo	'new man' – term applied to a man who became consul from a completely non-consular background
principes	'chief men' – legionaries in their prime of life forming the second line of a manipular legion of the middle Republic
princeps senatus	'chief of the Senate' – leading member of the Senate
socii	Latin and Italian allies of Rome
sufete	one of two annually elected chief magistrates of Carthage
suffectus	'substitute' – Roman consul elected to replace one who has died in office
triarii	'third-rank men' - veteran legionaries forming the third line of a manipular legion of the middle Republic
triplex acies	'triple line of battle' – threefold battle line of a Roman army
velites	'cloakwearers' – the youngest (and poorest) legionaries, who acted as lightly armed troops

INDEX